God
vs
Money

Other Books by the Author

The E-Giving Guide for Every Church
Not Your Parents' Offering Plate
Whose Offering Plate Is It?
The Church Money Manual
Rich Church, Poor Church

J. Clif Christopher

God
★ ★ VS ★ ★
Money

Winning Strategies in the Combat Zone

⬤) Abingdon Press™
Nashville

GOD VS MONEY:
WINNING STRATEGIES IN THE COMBAT ZONE

Copyright © 2018 by Abingdon Press

All rights reserved.

This book is printed on acid-free paper.

Library of Congress Cataloging-in-Publication Data has been requested.

978-1-5018-6811-5

18 19 20 21 22 23 24 25 26 27—10 9 8 7 6 5 4 3 2 1
MANUFACTURED IN THE UNITED STATES OF AMERICA

*To the men and women in the four incredible congregations
I served for twenty years, and to the soldiers with whom I was
proud to serve for eighteen years. I am who I am because of
all you taught me.*

★ ★ ★

Contents

★ ★ ★

Introduction

No one can serve two masters. . . . You cannot serve God and wealth.

Matthew 6:24

S everal years ago while sitting around with four men, all of whom were about my age, one of the men noted that all of us had sons who were graduating college and heading out to start their careers. He looked at all of us and said, "As I watched my son walk across the stage the other day with his diploma in hand I began to wonder what I would be seeing in my son when he is my age and watching his son walk across some stage. How would I like to describe him? What would he have become? What would his life be like?"

One of the other men jumped in and turned it back to him and said, "Well, what did you arrive at? What would you like to say about your son?"

"I think I just want to be able to say he has been successful," he replied. "He is going into marketing and has a good job with a good company. Who knows in thirty years where that will put him, but I hope he is successful. If he is then I think he will be happy."

Another opened up to the group, "You guys know what I am thinking. I would love to say that he has been inducted into the Hall of Fame. He reports to the Yankees minor league club next week. I think he has a chance, if he keeps hitting like he has been. Seriously, if he can just say he played for the Yankees it would make him so happy."

I jumped in next and made some comment about my hope being for my son to say he had been a good father who had done his best to raise good children. I felt that if a man could say that his kids had turned out well then he would be a happy man.

Finally, the last guy in our group spoke up, "I hope I can say that my son is a tither. If he has gotten his act together with how to give and realizes that all that he has belongs to God and not him, then he will have a foundation on life that few will have. Nothing would make me happier than to hear him say that he is a tither. I do not know if I would use the word *happy*, but I do believe that he will have had an abundant life."

The rest of us just stood there and I, for one, was left wishing I had said that. I believe that when we truly come to understand who we are and whose we are the first step toward a fulfilling life has been taken. We begin to learn that life is not about us, but about the One who created us. Life begins to order itself along the lines by which we were created. We develop an immunity to the incredible lures of the world crying out in a million different ways that real life comes from what we can get. Stuff becomes our pursuit, not God's kingdom, and stuff is a drug we are easily addicted to. It never satisfies. It constantly frustrates, and we find ourselves on a merry-go-round that gets us nowhere but just keeps going round and round.

God and money both made a lot of promises. God kept all of his and money kept none. But money has better advertising and we keep falling for it. We live in a society where God versus money is a daily battle. It is a war and right now we are not winning.

When one of our dads said, "I want my son to be a tither," he was saying "I want my son to be a winner." He wanted his son to be a real-life winner in a game that counts. What would you have said if asked this question? Would your first response be around behavior that exemplified Christ or would it be around salary, position, fame, or lifestyle? Right now you are probably thinking that you would give a wonderful answer based on Christian values, but is that exactly how you have raised your children? Is that what you are modeling for your children? Is that what you are praising in the media? Is that what they hear from you around the dinner table? Is that what you hear regularly being espoused in your church?

In this book I hope to lay out a life plan where those of us in church leadership can create persons who are capable of winning the war. These are the tools you are going to need to create persons who know how to go up against the lure of money and come out a victor on the other side. To some extent I hope this book becomes a training manual for pastors and church lay leaders to learn how to grow a congregation of generous persons who have been trained in how to give up control by stuff and let God have command of their lives.

We will explore what the realities are in today's society in trying to teach Christian stewardship and secure the funds for building up God's kingdom. We will focus on how donors think and why they choose or do not choose the church in their giving.

We will look at why giving to religion continues to fall to its lowest level in history. You will learn some tools and basics around simple church management in budget preparation and how to conduct successful campaigns and how to navigate through the strange world of finance.

We are going to talk about that mysterious phenomenon known as planned giving and why your church and your members need it. There will be sections on preaching on money and laying out a year-round program versus the standard three-week miracle approach in the fall.

It all will be brought not with the hope that you use these ideas to get more money, but that you can learn to shape more winners, true disciples of the Lord Jesus Christ, who know that what they have been given is infinitely more than anything they could ever give. I want us to create disciples who do not enter into this fight out of guilt or obligation, but out of a sincere belief that a life of generosity is a glorious life that leads to everlasting life, while a life of being controlled by stuff is a dead-end that destroys not only us but also the world around us. This needs to be a war we want to fight, not just one we have to fight.

Inside, you will find many references to how I see the importance of this fight versus a fight I was in back in the early 1990s as a member of the US Army. I am extraordinarily proud of serving for nearly twenty years and I learned a lot from the army about life and mission and focus. For those of you who get squeamish about war language, I can understand, but I do not apologize. I truly believe that we must take the attack upon our Christian values by a greedy, self-serving society very seriously. We must understand that they do not always play fair or nice. It is not pretty what this enemy is doing to our families and to our future. We must combat this threat now and not later. We must treat it like a war.

The war goes on. God versus money. I hope you and your people will wind up on God's side and be winners every day. Let's prepare for battle.

★ ★ ★

Chapter 1

The Combat Zone—
Area of Operation

*Whoever loves money never has enough; whoever loves wealth
is never satisfied with their income. This too is meaningless.
As goods increase, so do those who consume them. And what
benefit are they to the owners except to feast their eyes on them?*
Ecclesiastes 5:10-11 NIV

Back in 1991 I found myself on the other side of the world involved in the Gulf War. I was a chaplain assigned to a combat unit that eventually would be charged with leading the ground offensive into Iraq to force Saddam Hussein to pull his army out of Kuwait. Shortly after our arrival into Saudi Arabia, the Iraqis began to bombard us with Scud missiles. We learned that for some reason the missiles would begin around 5:00 in the afternoon and continue on into the night. We would huddle in various bunkers with gas masks on and await the eventual end to the onslaught. Few of us were seriously hurt, but one's nerves could get rattled and the constancy of it occurring night after night after night got very old. The attitude was that we must either give in to this or go fight this, but one way or the other we had to get it to stop. We chose to fight.

In today's world we are in a state of war with the constant bombardment of stuff. It pounds a message into our brains and into our hearts that is hard to resist. Many of us know that it is not exactly the answer, but its unending call continues to pulsate into our lives from television, magazines, and internet ads that seem to say this is the best alternative you have to fulfillment. We see the "beautiful people" with certain stuff and think that we too could be like them if we only drove a Lincoln or used Maybelline. Being like Clooney, or Jolie, or Pitt, or Brady or a Kardashian after all would be so much better than what I have right now. We either surrender in this battle or we fight. The realities are that Americans and the American church seem to be surrendering.

The area of operations of our combat zone has some important characteristics. It is important to understand the environment we are fighting in.

There are 324 million people in the United States so you can do the math on total monies spent.

These persons spend 32 percent on personal housing; 16 percent on transportation; 12 percent on food; 12 percent on insurance and pension; 8 percent on healthcare; 3 percent on clothing; 5 percent on entertainment; 3 percent on petty cash items; 7 percent on "other." Charity, education, and personal growth are lumped into "other."[1]

Intelligence Analysis—These persons do not place a very high priority on giving to persons beyond themselves except in rare circumstances. Generosity is not a core value.

They spend an average of $1,383 on Thanksgiving and Christmas food and gifts.[2]

They spend an average of $167 on jewelry.[3]

They spend an average of $327 on gambling.[4]

They spend $3,075 every second on pornography on the internet.[5]

Intelligence Analysis—These persons obviously have a lot of discretionary income that they chose to use in a variety of areas, many of which are not friendly to our cause.

George Barna in his book *America at the Crossroads* shares alarming statistics about the way the war is going for the hearts and minds of Americans. Surrender is all around us. He notes that only 45 percent of Americans go to worship at least once a month. This is the first time in American history that churchgoers are a minority of the population. Forty-six percent report being unchurched. This is up from 34 percent in 2000. Ten years ago, nearly 75 percent of Americans said they had made a personal commitment to Jesus Christ. Today that is down to 60 percent. Less than half of Americans believe the Bible holds the answers to a meaningful life.[6] Does this look like we are winning?

In describing what I have been referring to as a war, Barna shared this as a status report,

> The United States is in the early stages of biblical abandonment and the consequent cultural decline. Increasing numbers of persons are comfortable with faith as long as it provides the benefits they seek and is neither demanding nor constraining. Millennials...appear poised to wholeheartedly support the shift away from biblical Christianity and towards new belief patterns.[7]

Intelligence Analysis—The hearts and minds of the local population have largely been lost by our side. They have succumbed to the propaganda of the enemy.

From just a pure giving standpoint the statistics are frightening. "Giving to Religion" as a percentage of market share in charitable giving is down 42 percent from 1989 to 2014.[8] Where religion used to receive close to 60 percent of all charitable gifts, we now get 32 percent. Empty Tomb Inc. reports that gifts to congregations are down 27 percent since 1968 and gifts to missions are down nearly 50 percent.[9] We are a retreating army that is rapidly giving up territory.

Barna again shares alarming statistics. In 2014, 45 percent of Americans gave nothing to a church or other religious organization, up from 36 percent in 2004. One half of those donations averaged only $500, whereas in 2004, 5 percent of Americans tithed. A decade later that number is closer to 2 percent.[10] This statistic seems to be saying that though we still have a soldier or two, most do not want to fight anymore.

Intelligence Analysis—There have been several battles over the years and we have won a few, but the prevailing trends are that we will eventually lose this war to apathy and attrition.

None of this probably shocks any church leader today, but it should jar us to realize that there is a war on and so far we have not been fighting back very hard. My belief is that one of the ways we need to take on this scourge is to raise the focus on giving as not just an outcome of faith in Christ, but as a vehicle that can lead to greater faith in Christ. It has been attributed to Billy Graham that he once said, "The closest thing to a person's heart is their wallet." If we can help persons to surrender their dependence upon stuff they will soon learn to rely on God and give him control.

While in the army I spent several years working with basic training units. Young men and women would come scrambling off the bus on their first night of boot camp and would be met by an unyielding drill instructor (DI) who would get them into a line. The DI would demand they comply with where to drop their gear, how to stand, and when to move. These young people had blank stares on their faces, having no idea what had just hit them. It was all done with great intentionality—to make soldiers who would carry out the mission.

One of a DI's most important tasks is to strip away any notion that the recruit has any control. They were not going to control how they dress, eat, comb their hair, shower, call their mama, send a text, or much of anything else. For a seventeen- to twenty-year-old, this is often stoutly resisted. It is crucial if they are to function properly in an army unit involved in combat. It will not only help keep them alive but also contribute to the success of any operation. They absolutely must learn to follow the chain of command. The really great soldiers not only learn to follow but also soon realize and appreciate what following can mean to their lives. They begin to highly value it as a way of life.

Today's world fights against that mind-set. "You can have it all" is a slogan that resonates with today's young people. At your very fingertips you can control your music, communicate around the world, watch only what you want on video, open your door, start your car, and turn on your lights. You can be totally in control and you can do it with STUFF! The more stuff, the more control.

An old parable has it that a man was once walking along the edge of a mountain when he slipped. Soon he found himself dangling thousands of feet in the air holding on to a small, scraggly tree that sprouted from the rock. He began to yell for someone to save him. When that did not work he began to yell for God to save him. God answered, "Here I am. I will save you. Do you believe I will save you?" "Yes," was the answer. After a minute with nothing happening the man again yelled up to God and implored him to hurry and save him. God answered, "Here I am. I will save you. Do you believe I will save you?" "Yes" was again the answer. Nothing happened and, losing hope, the man cried out once again. God replied, "Let go of the limb."

For us to win this war, we are going to have to first let go of our stuff to understand how complete trust in God works. As long as we insist on hanging on to the tangible things like old trees, God cannot work miracles within us.

Is it faith first, and then we learn to give? Or is it give first, and then we develop faith? It can be either way and frankly I do not care which comes first. What must happen is that we eventually give up those things that are standing between us and the will of our heavenly Father to give us life and that life in abundance.

So this is where we are. Most of us are like raw recruits getting off the bus. You think you are hot stuff and you can conquer the world all by yourself. You will be reading new concepts and learning new ways to do things. Others of you have moved past the recruit stage and become a good soldier for Christ. What you need this book for is to train you to be a good drill instructor. You are going to be the one to follow these processes and principles to grow generous disciples of Jesus Christ so they can join his army and win this fight for the souls of humanity.

Questions for Review

1. In your church how prevalent is the love of money and stuff? Do you feel your church is doing better, worse, or about the same as other churches in warning persons of this threat?

2. Is *generosity* a word that is heard much from the pulpit or in classes?

3. What do you think the reaction in your church would be if you declare war against "stuff" and increase efforts to fight off its influence?

4. Do you ever see ways that a person's need to control harms your church?

★ ★ ★

Pastor as Drill Instructor

I appeal to you then, be imitators of me.
1 Corinthians 4:16

Last year while working at my desk I got a call from a finance team chairperson who wanted to talk with me about his pastor. He said that he and others on the team had been frustrated for some time that the pastor never addressed the issue of money from the pulpit. They had encouraged him and he would simply say that he weaves it into various sermons and prefers that to sermons directly on the topic of money in our lives. He went on to share that the pastor reluctantly engaged with the committee and got involved only when it appeared that there would be a shortfall of income. He mostly wanted the budget to balance and for his denominational obligations to be paid so he would not look bad to superiors. He righteously proclaimed quite often that he never looked at anyone's giving and thought that was something just between the giver and God. After all of this the chairperson got to the immediate issue, "Last night he called a committee meeting with us and the pastor's relation committee to share that he had gotten behind with the IRS and they now wanted payment of three years' taxes. We went over the numbers and it appears that he is about $30,000 in the hole. The IRS is pressuring him to square this obligation up. Anyway, he asked us to consider a short-term loan that would be taken from his salary over several years. I am calling you to see what your advice is on what we should do."

It is not important to know what advice I gave, but it is important to consider what position these church members had just been placed in. The teacher was coming to the students for assistance. The teacher was giving no leadership to those under his charge. This would have been like a drill instructor walking his young recruits over to the rappelling wall and saying that the ropes are laying over there, just tie them on, and see how it works while I go sit under this tree. Some of these recruits might die. Some of these church people will not discover what a generous life in Christ truly brings to one's life because their instructor (pastor) could not and would not lead.

Pastors and Disciple Leaders Must Model the Life of a Generous Disciple

The best drill instructors are not the ones who tell the recruit what to do, but model for them what to do. They tell the recruit to shine his shoes while wearing shined shoes. They tell the recruit to run two miles while running with them. They tell the recruit to show up for 5:00 formation while being there at 4:45. They model the life they preach about. This our pastors must do, especially in the areas where our people struggle the most—their dependence on stuff.

As pastors we have to model how we manage, spend, and give our money. Money is the chief enemy of the disciple-to-be. A pastor lives among the same temptations as his or her flock. He or she watches television and sees the same billboards that seek to influence all to want more and more and more. A pastor hears the same voices that praise those who have lake houses, fancy clothes, shiny cars, and take lavish vacations. Pastors are not immune to temptation, but through Christ they have learned a better way. It is this better way of living and giving that must be seen by the recruits.

I would see the drill instructors around the military installation going to the post exchange or commissary while off duty. Their uniforms looked just like they did when they were with the recruits early in the morning. Often, I would comment about how everything was perfectly put together and would get a reply, "I would have it no other way, sir." They were always teaching by modeling. For pastors this means we model the life of a generous disciple at Walmart, at a restaurant, at deer camp, or the movie theater. Wherever we are, we are called to set an example of what it means to have surrendered control to Jesus.

In my seminars I am frequently asked if a pastor should share his or her amount of giving with the congregation. The answer is a resounding YES! A leader must be seen and heard leading. Too many times I have heard pastors say that they will be supportive with their gifts, and that is all. What does that mean? How does that help me grow? I have heard persons say that they believe all persons should give proportionally. What is that? Is a penny a proportion? What coach, trainer, or drill instructor would use such ambiguous language? Not one who truly wanted to win!

Pastors should, at a minimum, put in print and share in worship exactly how they are trying to live out a Christian life of generosity. A testimony should always include how one came to determine what their giving would be. The pastor needs to share the journey and not just where he or she has arrived. It should be so clear that no one would misunderstand.

One of the most effective sermons I ever heard came from a pastor in an extremely large church. He rose, walked out in front of his people, and began by saying, "I have a confession to make." His confession was that when it came to generosity he had been a phony. He had either misled persons as to how he managed his money and his giving or he had been sure to keep it hidden. He went on to talk about how he got into debt with schooling, compounded that by trying to show a lifestyle like his first congregants had—on much less income—and just wasted one resource after another. Because he absolutely had spent more than what he had, he had been unable to give as he knew Christ would have him do. He was ashamed and embarrassed and on this day he came clean. No one in that audience was sleeping through this. Then he came out and said that beginning the previous week he was now ordering his financial life around the theme of grace and gratitude. He would put God first, not just on his lips but also with his wallet and his actions. He shared exactly what he was going to start giving and how he was going to shift things around to make that work. He shared how he intended to square up his debts and not create any new debt. He shared how thankful he was that God continued to love him even though, in so many ways he, the pastor, had been worshipping money more. He said he was grateful for the chance to be born again.

Now that was leadership!

Examine What Money Means to You

In our society it is proclaimed loudly that money and power go together. Most of us remember the infamous video of candidate Donald Trump proclaiming disgustingly how he could do just about anything he wanted to with women. When asked how he got away with it he said, "When you are rich they let you do anything." Why do you want money? What does it really do for you? Probably, your answer is not so you can molest someone, but is it so you can have security? Is it so you can exude a degree of success to those whose favor you value? Is it so you can have certain stuff that money can buy? My guess is that it is a lot more than you just want to feed and clothe your family. All of us need to have this conversation with ourselves and perhaps with a spiritual mentor.

Why do you feel uncomfortable talking about money? In my observations, money conversations are had far less often than conversations about sex or religion. I have been in serious conversations with numerous persons and groups about sexual ethics, practices, and the ways the Bible is interpreted regarding human sexual relationships. I have seen countless church signs proclaiming "Sex in Today's World" as the topic of the sermon on Sunday. I have heard pastors proclaim that next Sunday they would be discussing "Sex in Relationships," and families may want to consider whether to bring children or not. These sermon series often are the most crowded of any all year long.

.   I have sat around many a dinner table talking about individual religious beliefs. The question, "How do you think God might view this or that?" is asked by me and to me with friends. We talk prayer, religion, worship preferences, sacraments, observances, and all manner of things regarding our individual churches. But I seldom, if ever, see or hear this about money.

Few pastors would put a sign on the front lawn announcing that next Sunday he or she is going to preach about "Money in Our Lives." If he or she shares from the pulpit a week ahead of time it is probably so those who do not want to hear it can just stay away rather than come and complain. At the Thanksgiving dinner table you would be kicked under the table if you tried to raise a question about how much money we make and how we should be more generous to others. Even with our children we discuss religion openly and often persuasively. As they approach puberty we open the door to discussions about sexual feelings and sexual behavior. But quite often we never get around to having any discussion with those under our charge about money and the destructive lure that it can be. What is the role of money in your life? Answering this question is the first place a leader must go.

A good friend asked me for a reference to a financial advisor. I gave him the name of a wonderful Christian man I had great trust in. My friend's next question was, "Will he take a guy like me?" I said, "What do you mean?" and he replied, "Will he take a guy like me who is not very wealthy, but just needs some advice?"

Money is often associated with our sense of self-worth. Deep down we think we will be a bit more special if we just had a bit more money. It is the amount of money that in our heart of hearts defines for us who we are.

One guy I have known for years said to me just the other day, "My advisor called me after this big stock rally and told me that as of today I was a millionaire. He said congratulations. Can you believe it? After all these years of working I finally made it to be a millionaire." To my friend this was a check mark that validated him to himself. He had been a great friend for years. He had raised a great family and been a hard worker. But now he hit a financial level that made him "somebody." Where are you?

I talked with a woman once who said that she slept each night with a short-barreled twelve-gauge shotgun right beside her bed. She said it made her feel secure. What makes you feel secure at night? Are you secure in knowing that Jesus Christ died for you and that you have been forgiven of your sins, destined for eternal life if anything were to happen to you? Do you feel secure knowing that this world is not ultimately in your hands or in the hands of any other human being, but in God? Do you feel secure in knowing that neither death nor life, nor angels, nor rulers, nor things present or things to come, nor powers, nor height, nor depth, nor anything else in all creation, will be able to separate you from the love of God in Christ Jesus (Romans 8:38-39)?

Or do you feel secure if the market went up, or your long-term debt has been paid, or you got a raise, or someone just gave you a significant financial gift? Which makes you feel more secure?

If we are ever going to lead our troops into battle and be effective, we have to first come to grips with which side we truly want to be on. God or money—which one ultimately has the answers to life's mysteries for you? Which one is going to bring you the life for which you have always aspired? I know what your Sunday school teacher said in the lesson, but what have you taken into your heart? A good drill instructor does not teach and teach and teach his troops because it says so on page ten of the DI manual. The best ones believe it deep down in their beings that what they are teaching is the best way for a soldier to perform and live. A recruit can tell the difference.

Now I would be greatly remiss if I left the impression that the pastor (drill instructor) can lead by himself or herself. No one is more important, but laity (fellow recruits) must also be willing to pick up the mantle. No one motivates better than a peer. When a fellow recruit gets out front and encourages compatriots to follow, the troops take notice. When they exalt, "You can do it and I will show you how," others listen. It is one thing for a coach to suggest that players come in early or stay late, but when one of the players announces that he or she will be there early and stay late—now that gets attention.

For the church to become the generous community that Christ desires, there must be laity willing to step forward and lead in announcing their commitment. They must stand in front of the congregation or a Sunday school class and invite persons to follow them. They must share their stories as to how generosity is a priority in their Christian walk that keeps them grounded and close to Christ—even with mortgages, college educations, retirement plans, and family sickness.

When Is the Best Time?

Many of the church leaders reading this have already begun to think about becoming the leader your recruits need you to be.

You know they need an example to follow. You know they need to hear a dynamic witness about having security in Christ and casting off the false promises of money. You know that more members of your congregation suffer from the sin of loving money more than they suffer from the sin of loving someone else's spouse, love of alcohol, or any number of easy-to-see sins. Yes, your people love money more than God and you know it. So when do you start to lead them away from their sin and back to life in Christ? Today!

Today is the best day to decide that you have to get your life right before you can help others get theirs right. You have to find a way to have your house in order before you discuss the need for them to get their houses in order. Today is the best day to decide to get debt's dominance out of your life. You may need a good financial or credit counselor, or you may be able to make a plan yourself. But do it today.

Today is the best day to decide to begin giving in a way that reflects gratitude and grace. Today is the best day to determine that the one debt you have to fix is the debt to God. Maybe you have to sell something. Maybe you have to downsize your vehicle? Maybe you have to decide not to take any vacations away from home. Maybe you change the way you shop for clothes or how often you eat out. Maybe you change your giving habits on birthdays, anniversaries, and holidays. But, one way or another, make your giving to God a priority.

Going cold turkey like this will not be easy but it is necessary. After some time you should be able to maintain your priority of God first and add in some joy with a vacation and some gifts, but for now—you are paying off old debts.

Questions for Review

1. When you read that you must model what it means to be a generous disciple, how does that make you feel?

2. Do you find yourself ever worrying about having enough money, or do you spend more time being thankful for the money you do have?

3. Can you write a paragraph about what money means to you today? Have your feelings about money changed over the years?

4. Should a pastor have a different attitude about money than laypersons? Should a pastor and lay leaders be held to the same accountability standard?

5. How would you feel if your pastor said he or she did not tithe? What if he or she did not give at all? What if a Sunday school teacher said the same thing?

★ ★ ★

C h a p t e r   3

Join Up or Conscientiously Object—What Is Right?

Then God said, "Let us make humankind in our image, accord-ing to our likeness; and let them have dominion over the fish of the sea, and the birds of the air, and over the cattle, and over all the wild animals of the earth, and over every creeping thing that creeps upon the earth." So God created humankind....
Genesis 1:26-27 NRSV

The mission statement of the US Army states, "As a branch of the armed forces, the mission of the US Army is to fight and win our Nation's wars, by providing prompt, sustained land dominance, across the full range of military operations and the spectrum of conflict, in support of combatant commanders." When someone volunteers to be in this army this is what they are volunteering to do. It is clear from the beginning. No one tries to surprise a recruit with what it means to wear "US Army" on your uniform. You may be called upon to fight and win a war.

Now there are some outstanding persons in our society who do not believe that fighting in the army is an appropriate thing to do. They arrived at this conclusion after significant forethought and perhaps even prayer and did not volunteer. Our country, in its wisdom, gives everyone that opportunity.

But, if you do sign up, then fighting for the nation may well be something you will be called upon to do and refusing to do so at that time can be a punishable offense. You really could not have an effective army any other way. What would it be like if the president had to actually wonder how many might show up if he declares an emergency? How would a unit ever get its act together on time if first the commanders had to sit down and discuss with each soldier whether they wanted to go? No, when you put on the uniform you know full well what it means and what the mission is. It is assumed you have already thought through what is right for you. As you continue reading this book on winning the war for the souls of persons through generosity, I hope all of you have thought through, theologically, what the mission is.

A Theology of Stewardship

Way back in 1985 I was invited to join the US Army Reserve. Over a long period of study, prayer, and talking with colleagues I chose to take the oath. I served through Desert Shield, Desert Storm, and 9/11. It was the right thing for me to do and I feel very good about my service. I would never tell anyone else that it was the right thing for him or her to do. Many of the churches I work with today do not believe that military service is within God's will. I have enormous respect for their convictions. They arrived at that through the same process that I arrived at my decision. I joined up and they chose to conscientiously object. What we did in coming to our conclusions is called *theology* taken from the words *theos* (God) and *logos* (knowledge). From our knowledge of God we found our answer and our calling.

Likewise, I would never say to someone that they "must" be generous or that I know God "commands" them to give in a certain way. I, for instance, would never have told the rich ruler that he should sell everything he had and give to the poor. It was, as Jesus knew, exactly what this man needed to experience the fullness of life in communion with God. I would ask everyone, however, to do what the rich ruler was doing—and that is seek out the will of God in earnest and then make a decision on how you are to practice generosity. Way too many times, our addiction to self never lets God get a word in on what is right for us.

My theology begins and ends with the notion that our God is the Creator and Owner of all the good things in the world. It was, is, and always will be his! In his infinite wisdom he chose to give us "dominion" over what is his. He placed his world into our hands to manage in ways that would be pleasing and glorifying to him. He did not want to be left out of the equation but wanted us to be the managers who would use those gifts to bring the world to him and remain within him forevermore. My biggest problem is waking up every day and hearing the siren call, "It Is Mine." Money and other stuff call me like the serpent to Eve, that if I have just a little bit more, then I too will be like God. Like an addict, I am attracted to the thought and I venture forth to acquire a bit more. For a short period it works and I feel the high of a new thing, only to have it wear off and be replaced by a new craving promising to work better than the "stuff" before it.

Years ago, a good friend loaned me his boat so I could go on a fishing trip with several others. I got my instructions about the boat and the motor from my friend and sought to be extremely conscious of all that he said in how to take care of it. I trailered it with great care, and parked it on secure level ground. I wanted to do everything with it my friend would have done. The next morning, I trimmed the motor just as he said. I made sure the drain plug was in nice and tight. I launched it with another's help, being sure not to hit anything with the trailer. Then disaster struck. I found myself in a crosswind in a small launch area. There were numerous boats and several docks nearby. I tried to pump the brake, but there was no brake. I quickly shifted into reverse only to swing the boat in exactly the wrong direction. I was headed for the metal corner of a protruding dock and I just froze. The boat rammed broadside into the piling and a chunk of fiberglass gave way the size of a softball. I was devastated, but not because the boat would sink. It would not. It was not that it couldn't be repaired. It could. It was that I had accepted a gift of the use of my friend's boat and I had not treated it with the same degree of care he would have. I got in a hurry. I did not properly consider the circumstances and now I had to go look at my friend and share with him what I had done to his gorgeous boat.

God has loaned me his world. It is he who has given me the air I breathe, the trees I see changing colors, the fish I catch on a lazy Saturday, the food I eat throughout the day, and the money I carry in my wallet. IT IS HIS! My theology tells me that I am to treat all that is his as he would and not as I may wish. The problem is that I forget. The media tells me that I can have it all—that I may borrow all from God. The media tells me that it is okay to eat of the fruit so I too can be like God. This job is mine! This land is mine! This car is mine! My family is mine! The air I breathe, the clothes I wear, the body I use—all are mine! This is blasphemy.

Without the discipline of being generous, I will only fall deeper and deeper into this trap that I believe will rob me of the life God intended, not fulfill my life. Following the loud voices of consumption will lead to frustration and discontent and moral laxity. Being spiritually generous is the vaccine I take against these demons.

There are days I wish we had to put on a Christian uniform to remind us that we belong to something far greater than ourselves. My army uniform had emblazoned across the chest—"US Army." There are patches on the sleeves reminding me of the units for which I am responsible. It is very hard to walk around in that uniform, hat and all, and forget you are a soldier whose job it is to serve the nation in the army. As a Christian I dress like everyone else. The generous and the selfish—the believer and the nonbeliever—are indiscernible. I can hide and easily forget whose I am, and what my job is. I can become my own god quite easily.

I believe that Christian stewardship is the reason we were created. It is to be our vocation. We have been placed on this earth to be a part of God's mission of caring, being generous, and doing justice. We are to care, give, and serve as God would do. We are to raise our families with this understanding of stewardship. We are to perform our jobs with this understanding of stewardship. We are to treat others with this understanding of stewardship, and we are to give of our resources and talents with this understanding of stewardship. This is our ultimate mission. We are to be first and foremost stewards.

The US Army has what is called the "warrior ethos" and the first part of this four-part ethos says, "I will always put mission first." When you wear that uniform you come to understand how mission outranks everything else. A soldier in a combat environment eats, sleeps, dresses, combs his hair, and brushes his teeth around what is necessary for the accomplishment of the mission. As a Christian, I feel I am called to place my job as a steward above all. My primary job is not to be father, husband, employer, fisherman, or consumer. My primary reason *to be* is to be a steward of all that God has given me. That is the purpose of my creation and when that awareness dominates my thinking, life is ordered as God would have it to be ordered. What does God want me to do with the family that he gave me? What does God want me to do with the job he has given me? What does God want me to do with the creatures in the river? What does God want me to do with the income I get twice a month? Answering these questions is my understanding of how to make sense of life and my purpose in it.

One of the frustrating parts of being in the army is the early awareness that this is not a democratic institution. All voices are not equal. Everyone has a right to complain, but only the commander has the right to command—and once the commander has spoken that is the end of it. An army just cannot function on the battlefield if it has to stop and vote every time a major decision is being made. We did not always like it, but we knew that following command was our best chance of having success.

There is only one Creator and it is not you or me. There is only One who took nothing and created something. I have witnessed a commander lock the heels of a young soldier and spell out to him how the chain of command worked and how that young soldier was at the bottom and not the top of the chain, but none did it as superbly as God did with Job in chapter 38 of this great book:

Gird up you loins like a man. I will question you and you will declare to me. Where were you when I laid the foundation of the earth? Tell me, if you have understanding. Who determined its measurements, surely you know!...Have you commanded the morning since your days began, and caused the dawn to know its place, so that it might take hold of the skirts of the earth, and the wicked be shaken out of it?...Have you comprehended the expanse of the earth? Declare, if you know all this. (Job 38:3-18 NSRV)

It goes on and on and on. I can only imagine how Job felt while he was locked up tight having to listen to God explain to him the realities of being the Creator and the created. It was not pretty. Job's job was not to be doing God's job. God had that spot taken. Job's job was to be doing what he had been created to do and that was to be the steward or servant of God. I think God made that pretty clear in this chapter. We are no different than Job. Stewardship is our job!

I could go on and on about what I believe is the proper relationship between myself and God, but what is more important than hearing where I am, is you discovering where you are. The recruiting poster is saying that God wants you to come and be his steward. Do you feel you need to sign up or do you object? Do the theological work to arrive at your answer and then remain true to the understanding of what it is to be the created.

Questions for Review

1. How would you define your mission in life?

2. Do you ever struggle with the notion that what you see, touch, feel, and put in your wallet is not really yours?

3. Would you have a different attitude about life if you were more conscious that you are just looking after it for God versus owning it outright?

4. How many persons in your church could express a definition of stewardship?

★ ★ ★

Chapter 4

The Rules of Engagement

*Teach and urge these duties.... Those who want to be rich fall
into temptation and are trapped by many senseless and harm-
ful desires that plunge people into ruin and destruction. For
the love of money is the root of all kinds of evil, and in their
eagerness to be rich some have wandered away from the faith
and pierced themselves with many pains.*

1 Timothy 6:2-10 NRSV

I n the military it is called "rules of engagement." What are the
guiding rules by which we shall engage the enemy? Under
what circumstances shall we become fully engaged to accom-
plish the mission and when should the army hold back due to
certain factors? Commanders dutifully follow the rules of engagement and teach and preach it to their subordinates. When those
rules are clear and concise they can be a strong contributing factor
in leading an army to victory. There should be no ambiguity!

One woman spoke to her friend, "What did the pastor talk
about last Sunday?" "He spoke on sin," was the answer. "Was he
for it or against it?" the lady replied. There should be no ambiguity

in our preaching, but often, out of fear of complaint, too many preachers try to sound like politicians who want to see if they can please everybody. Our incomes depend upon the voluntary support of a congregation. If you upset too many members of a congregation, you can be fired or moved. Deep down, all pastors know this. Sermons on being prayerful or being forgiven or being loved come easily and often from our pulpits, but sermons on societal ethics, guns, homosexuality, race relations, or gambling are not heard very often. Is it because we do not think God has an opinion or because we know our members have diverse opinions?

I was once the pastor of a church that was located about two miles from a large regional gambling establishment. This establishment put in a lot of tax dollars for the community, hired several hundred people, and was the primary support of several nonprofits in the area. Early on in my ministry there, a church member came up to me and said, "Pastor, you know we have members who sit on the board at (the gambling establishment). Now, we all expect our pastor to be against gambling, but it would be unwise for you to ever voice it." They were trying to be helpful to me and establish the rules of engagement with the congregation so I would not get in hot water. But should my rules come from this source? Were the members my commander in chief, or were they to be the soldiers I was to train (however reluctant they may be to training)? Only I could decide.

In every church I served I was warned about talking too much about money. "Our last pastor talked way too much about money, and it really got him in trouble." "We do not want persons to think that all we are interested in is their money." "Seems like all we ever hear about is money." "If you will just stay away from money in the pulpit, most everybody will be happy."

We live in a society that is not dedicated to following Christ as Lord. This society is constantly trying to find another way to "eat of the fruit" and "be like God." This is what we are at war with. George Barna found that 70 percent of Americans believe that they can "have it all." They can have great jobs and great families and not need to sacrifice anything of their personal desires.[1] Media continues to bombard us with a message that with just a bit more money, the right clothes on, the right perfume, driving a certain car, or vacationing in this certain spot will be the final piece of the puzzle that makes life complete. None of this fits the gospel.

Paul warned his young preacher, Timothy, of just this kind of mind-set and urged him to preach and teach against it. He knew that persons were standing way too close to the mountain edge and urged his pastors to preach another way before destruction beset them. He urged them to do it because he loved them and knew that God loved them and what they were doing was ruinous and would lead to death and not life. Paul was setting his rules of engagement.

It is very interesting in reading about both Jesus's and Paul's admonitions to their followers. Neither urged a lot of preaching and teaching against skipping worship, or drinking too much, or betraying a spouse, or being angry, or stealing, even though all are mentioned and cautioned against. What both of them did over and over and over was warn the disciples and "disciples-to-be" about the potential for money, riches, and stuff to destroy lives. We could fill this book up with biblical quotes plainly and boldly warning persons about how stuff was going to be the great tempter of their lives and nothing overshadowed wealth in its capacity to destroy one's soul. Most of us, clergy and laity alike, have heard, and can even quote, many of these "rules of engagement." Why do we not follow the rules of Jesus as much as the rules of society in our preaching?

Again I share a depressing word from George Barna's book on current trends:

> Christians will have a golden opportunity to lead the way in a society that is losing its sense of direction and purpose.... Unfortunately, assuming that current attitudinal and behavioral patterns persist, it is more likely that Christians will follow rather than lead in this regard and accept the dominant perspectives on success and the most common and popular path thought to lead to success. In other words, Christians are more likely to settle for the dominant cultural alternative rather than heed biblical exhortations to work as if they are serving God Himself and thereby realize success through obedience to His commands and principles. In doing so, Christians are in danger of both dishonoring God and failing American society.[2]

We must engage from the pulpit now and do so boldly and without hesitation or compromise.

Generosity Must Be Proclaimed and Seen as a Core Value

How would persons in your church describe generosity? Would they say that you always meet the budget? Would they say that you help feed the poor at a downtown mission? Would they say that you usually meet your denominational obligations? Would they say you raised a lot of money and built a building three years ago?

What I would hope they would say is that they know they are a blessed community that has been given countless gifts by their Creator to be used for his glory and the betterment of the world. They should be talking about how conscious they are of the need to give and how desirous they are to have the opportunity to give because so much has been given them. They should be talking much more about how they have been spiritually blessed as they have given than how the church has met its obligation of paying its bills. If I hear these things from laypersons in the pew then I know they understand generosity and what being a follower of Christ is all about. I will see them rejoicing at the lives that have been changed by these gifts not the money they "gave up." I will know this is a church that has been taught by its leaders who were not afraid of engaging as Christ would have us do.

Just this past week I opened up an email newsletter from a church to find the opening line of the pastor's remarks, "This Sunday is our annual stewardship Sunday. We will be talking about our budget for next year and how every family can help us meet our needs in the coming year. I hope all of you will be present." Now this seems rather innocent doesn't it? It is something that probably thousands of churches have put out in the fall of the year. No church member is going to call and complain about this. After all, even the greatest cynic would not complain at this. A church must have money to stay open. They applaud this rule of engagement. But it sends a terrible message that will not lead to us winning the battle.

This simple message conveys that financial stewardship is something we should give serious thought to one Sunday a year. It is not a core value all year long. It is not a way of life. It is a vehicle to help pay the bills. The rules of engagement are that you do discuss this once every fifty-two Sundays and avoid it at all others times. It is not mentioned in regard to how we should run our businesses. It is not mentioned in how we should prioritize things with our families. It is not mentioned in how we should recreate. It is not mentioned in regard to how we live most of our lives. The rules are that it can be discussed once a year and then only as necessary.

A couple of years ago I was invited to preach in a church I knew well on what they called their "Stewardship Sunday." I really did not want to do it because I think having a guest preacher once a year to discuss this topic is highly ineffective. It also sends a message that the pastor does not think this is very important, otherwise he or she would be addressing it. Therefore, the audience is generally tuned out and present only because they had nothing else planned for that one hour of the week. But against my better judgment, I accepted the invitation and I preached. I was a bit selfish in this acceptance because it was a large church with a beautiful sanctuary and I had long wanted to preach there. Anyway, at the conclusion of my sermon challenging the members to a higher level of discipleship exemplified by their generosity, the pastor stood to conclude the service saying, "I want to thank Dr. Christopher for his message this morning and to say that I am so glad he delivered that message since I sure did not want to do it." The congregation laughed and I wanted to cry. What they just heard was that Dr. Christopher is urging you to a place and a response that you do not have to take seriously. Her rules of engagement were that, when it comes to this topic, she will not engage.

Another Sunday, I was in a church visiting as I often do while on the road, and the pastor announced that he would be talking about money next week, so anyone who did not want to hear it has been duly warned in advance. The congregation laughed. His rules of engagement were that if money is involved proceed with great caution and warn the enemy (those in love with stuff) in advance so that none are severely affected by future actions so as to negate retaliatory behavior.

In yet another worship service, the lay chair of the finance committee stood in the pulpit to share how the budget was going to be cut if more gifts did not come in within the next two weeks. He shared some figures that depressed everyone and then spelled out the ministries that would be cut. He also said this, which I remember the most, "I know no one wants to hear about money, but we are a business, and we need money to run." The rules of engagement are that if things get dire and catastrophe is around the corner, you should engage only to the degree that stems the attack and then resort to prior behavior.

The Recommended Rules of Engagement

First, clearly identify the enemy that is attacking you. Do not just blindly strike out. The enemy is sin! It is a sin to put anything before the Lord our God. It is a sin to want to be God. It is a sin to think we can control our world by ourselves. It is a sin to place confidence in our ability to have stuff over our trust in God. This is your congregation's greatest sin. You may have persons involved in adultery, but probably not many. You may have persons who have to gamble every week, but probably not many. You may have persons who rely on alcohol to get them through the day, but probably not many. You may have a thief, but probably not many.

However, a great majority of your congregation loves stuff and money more than they love God. They spend their life trying to build one more barn. They have frantic days seeking to add more to a 401(k). They desperately want to own a house on the lake, thinking that if they only had one then all their weekends would have peace and joy. It consumes them. This is sin! My friend Bill Easum once said to me, "Never apologize for seeking to separate persons from that which they love more than God." That is the rule of engagement for Christians. We preach to separate persons from that which they love more than God. That is one of our leading rules of engagement.

Our rule of engagement is that where we see sin, we attack it from as many fronts as is necessary to defeat it so that God's kingdom may come upon the earth. Preaching is one of the most powerful and necessary ways that we fight the fight.

We must preach on the spiritual power of generosity, not on raising money. We must lift up numerous times throughout the year the danger that stuff can impose on us. Persons should hear the need for generosity and discipline in January as they are thinking of new life in a new year. Throughout Lent they should hear of the need for generosity as they equate their sacrifice with that of Jesus as he headed toward Jerusalem. They should hear of generosity as a great fruit of our relationship with God as they enter into Pentecost. They should hear how differently we cheerful Christians give versus how they are giving on April 15. They must hear a counter-message to consumerism as they go into the summer with big expensive vacations looming. They need to hear, as my friend Mike Slaughter says, that "Christmas is not THEIR birthday" going through Advent. At a bare minimum I believe if we are to counter an enemy that sells the message that stuff saves, then we have to clearly do so at least six times a year. Our rule of engagement is that we will take on the enemy at least six out of fifty-two Sundays, and that no one who is present will misunderstand what we are shooting at. The goal here is always to change lives and behaviors, not raise money. It is crucial that this be heard by all present. If they hear that money is the endgame, then the victory will be hollow and not last.

Some of you will remember the country song that Chris Janson came out with a few years ago called "Buy Me a Boat." It is a perfect song for someone to take and do a lesson or sermon around.

In the song, he notes that he wishes he had a rich uncle or he was as rich as Warren Buffet. He then shifts to preaching a bit, saying that he knows it is said that money cannot buy happiness and is the root of all evil, even noting that a camel cannot get through the eye of the needle. "Money can't buy everything," he says. "But it could buy me a boat!"[3] Then he throws in some more toys he could buy like a Yeti cooler, a new truck, and a couple of million bucks to play with. In so many ways, this is a great song with a lot to teach us—and our people who have bought a lot of boats and trucks, hoping that happiness and fulfillment is around the corner.

I really like listening to that song, and I bought it for my playlist. I contributed to Chris Janson being worth a couple of million bucks. But this is stewardship heresy. It absolutely defines the enemy for us. Our soldiers for Christ know that it says money is the root of all evil and that it sounds cool...BUT it could buy them a boat and a boat is exactly what one needs to make life work out just like I want it. A boat, a Yeti 110, a new truck, and a couple of million dollars. Is there any better answer to having a fulfilling life? Our rule of engagement says that we should play this song. Get well acquainted with the strategy of our opponent and then with a loud and convincing voice. Attack! Attack! Attack! Preach it!

Questions for Review

1. How do you feel about sermons related to money or our worship of stuff?

2. In your church do you hear too many sermons on money or not enough? How would most persons answer this question? Why?

3. When looking at the words to Chris Janson's song, do you feel this expresses your church members' attitudes about stewardship or not? What about your attitude?

4. Why is it that most of us can quote the scriptures related to money, just as Janson could, but we still think we need "a boat," "a couple of million dollars," or just more stuff?

★ ★ ★

C h a p t e r   5

Winning Sure Beats Losing

Let us run with perseverance the race that is set before us,
looking to Jesus the pioneer and perfecter of our faith.
Hebrews 12:1-2 NRSV

The days of winning coming easy have passed us by. No longer is the church the primary influencer in society. No longer do the majority of Americans listen to sermons or read the Bible as the primary sources for guidance in behavior. No longer are Sunday mornings or Wednesday nights reserved solely for church people to use. No longer are most businesses closed on a Sunday. No longer do generous Americans blindly give to their houses of worship with complete confidence that the gift will be well used appropriately. The battlefield that we fight on has been altered dramatically. Because of that we find that many churches are losing people and, at an even faster rate, losing funds for ministry. You cannot win if you bring a knife to a gunfight. You will lose if you show up with a horse and the other side has tanks. For way too many of us, we are trying to do combat with a twenty-first-century opponent using twentieth-century tools.

The great church strategist Lyle Schaller stated in one of his last works, *The New Context for Ministry*, "This new face of American philanthropy is distinguished by an unprecedented competition of the charitable dollar. For well over 90% of all Christian congregations... this means they will NOT be able to compete...."[1]

So how do we compete so that we win instead of lose? I know that in many circles, church leaders dislike the idea of competing. I get it. It can feel like combat sometimes and no one really likes combat, but if you have to go into combat, then winning sure beats losing! If you do not compete, then the church loses. If you compete badly, the church loses. You can sit on your righteous high horse all day long, but the mission will fail, disciples will not be made, children will not be taught, the lost will not be saved, the hungry will not be fed, and Jesus will not be known. But you stayed out of the foxhole and refused to compete. Who is the real winner now?

Raise the Level of Expectation for Spiritual Training

Every soldier in the army is expected to pass a physical fitness test every year, or in some cases every six months. When I was a soldier, that test consisted of doing a certain number of push-ups and sit-ups in two minutes and running two miles within a certain time. These expectations were published and all of us knew what they were long before we sought to meet them. Special operators have an even higher level of expectations and these too are published ahead of time. Fail to live up to the standard and you can and will be removed from the army. Within the church, I believe we need to list what the expectations are for spiritual training. What should a disciple be expected to do so as to perform the mission of ushering in God's kingdom?

One of the most asked questions I get is about starting a new church and what I feel is the most important thing to do. My answer for years has been that if I were starting one today I would make sure it was a high-expectation church. It would be a church where persons understood long before they affiliated formally what was expected from a disciple of Jesus Christ. I would not expect perfect people, but I would lay out a series of expectations that were measurable, which I considered biblical in being a disciple of Christ. All would be expected to grow every day and none would think that membership was the medal stand. Persons would know what a disciple was expected to be and given the tools to arm themselves as best as possible to do combat against a sinful world.

Jesus seemed to have this in mind in the Gospel of Luke, chapter 14, when he discussed the cost of discipleship. As you might remember, he had large crowds following him. Most of us would have settled for this (big membership, high attendance). However, it says he turned to them and said, "Whoever comes to me and does not hate father and mother, wife and children, brothers and sisters, yes, and even life itself, cannot be my disciple. Whoever does not carry the cross cannot be my disciple…consider the cost…none of you can become my disciples if you do not give up all of your possessions" (14:25-33).

We have been recruiting an army of people to be the hands and feet of Christ and never letting them know there is much more to it than what they see on the recruiting poster. We have tended to bring persons into membership with absolutely no idea of what discipleship is all about. We have been grossly negligent in laying out expectations for prayer or worship, study, service, evangelism, or giving. We have just added names to the roll and in many cases this has proven to be far more of a hindrance than a help. Jesus was adamant that he did not want a "ghost" army. He did not relish in a bunch of Jesus groupies. He wanted persons who understood that they were tasked with carrying out the will of the Lord God Almighty, Creator of the universe. They would be the ones upon whom the success of his plan would rest. They would be the ones to whom God would give all the means to bring peace on earth, feed the poor, clothe the naked, and free persons from oppression. They were to be God's mighty army. But, most church members today have no idea of these expectations. They are there for fellowship and friendship. If the going gets tough, they will just let God fight the fight alone.

This is why in one church, as in many, they told me that 75 percent of all new confirmands (youth brought into membership after a series of classes) never show in church again. This is why in most established churches today 50 percent of the members give absolutely nothing. This is why the average worship attendance in America hovers around 40 percent. The army of the church has recruited a bunch of soldiers who have no intention of going into battle for the gospel. We are getting back exactly what we have led persons to believe is expected. Not much!

When my army unit was called upon to lead the way in the ground invasion of the Gulf War, the biggest surprise we encountered was not a weapon system or particular tactic. The biggest surprise we got from the enemy was that most wanted to surrender without ever firing a shot. As we approached with our tanks they were scrambling out of their trenches and armored vehicles waving white flags and holding up their hands. We had to pause our advance to deal with so many POWs. Is this not an image of the church today? As society moves further and further away from the values of faith and family, the church seems to be seeking a way to surrender just to save our life (building, job, tradition). If we are going to win then we have to raise the level of expectations of what a disciple is to be in the twenty-first century and not just around giving, but discipleship. You will have a smaller army, but a much more capable one.

We must begin before people join to instruct them concretely on expectations.

Spiritual Training Expectations

1. A disciple of Jesus Christ at First Church is expected to be in worship every Sunday they are healthy and able. If unable to be present at this church, they should be in worship, if at all possible, where they are. Worship is a vital discipline to helping us maintain a healthy relationship with Christ.

2. A disciple of Jesus Christ at First Church is expected to spend time every day in prayer for the church and for the church family. A regular and disciplined prayer life is absolutely necessary for us to stay in proper alignment with God and his will for our lives.

3. A disciple of Jesus Christ at First Church is expected to share his or her faith with family, friends, and acquaintances on a regular basis. This should never be intrusive, but done in caring and loving ways so that others who do not know Jesus might come to see his grace in your life. It is expected that you will bring persons to worship and

other church opportunities that an even larger witness to the Christian community may be experienced. Learning how to witness and doing so is a gift we share with those who do not know the joys in Christ that we do. Not doing it is selfish and designed to keep Christ to ourselves. That is the quickest way to lose that same relationship.

4. A disciple of Jesus Christ at First Church is expected to spend numerous days and hours in service to those outside our church community. This mission service may be done in overseas missions or local missions. It may include feeding the hungry, clothing the naked, visiting the prisoner, building homes for the homeless, curing the sick, visiting the lonely, or any number of other opportunities where the love of Christ needs to be manifest to those who are isolated or lost or hurting. If we truly hope to find life we must be willing to lose our life in others.

5. A disciple of Jesus Christ at First Church is expected to give at least a tithe (10 percent) of one's income to the church and make financial offerings in support of other good works as they feel led. Our Lord was well aware of the lure of money to dominate our lives, and by the giving of money in a disciplined and systematic way, the disciple is building up a defense against this threat to the relationship with Christ.

At First Church we know that our relationship with Christ comes through God's grace and our faith in that grace. It is not dependent upon our doing anything. However, as in any relationship this love is strengthened and nourished by disciplined spiritual practices that all disciples should follow. The above expectations are our way of helping all be spiritually fit.

As persons seek membership into the church they are instructed in the foundations above and offered the opportunity to sign a covenant to such with a pastor. Within this covenant may be a plan of action to assist the disciple to grow and mature in each area. The pastor or lay mentor then works with the new disciple and the covenant throughout the initial year to live into their contract with the Lord.

Now be prepared! You will find that the enemy will consider this a serious threat. There will be significant resistance from those church members who liked the "Boy Scout" or "Country Club" rules better than the rules of this army of disciples. When Jesus made it clear that persons would not be welcome who just wanted to hang around for the fellowship of it, but instead would need to prioritize his mission in their life and be willing to sacrifice on a cross, he lost a lot of followers. However, the army he had left went on to change the world. You will be accused of not loving all persons or not practicing grace, and that is simply not true. You are trying to help usher in God's kingdom and to do that, it is going to take a lot more effort than saying "pretty please." You are going to need an army of disciples committed to the cause of Christ like the world has never seen. You start developing this army long before its members raise their right hands and take the oath.

Officers to Lead the Troops

In every organization the frontline workers look to their supervisors—trainers, bosses, officers—to reflect what the work is really about. Within the army these are the officers and the non-commissioned officers (sergeants). Under them are all the troops.

These troops are not as developed in their understanding of the "army way." They do not know the dangers or the opportunities. Without leadership many may be lost in combat. In the study of combat over the years it is easily seen that the winner was often the one with the best leaders. They made the right decision at the right time for the right reason and victory was the result. Losers, on the other hand, had less committed leadership incapable of carrying out the mission or often not even dedicated to it. You will see quite often that a decision was made that benefited the leader to the detriment of the troops and the mission.

Within the church it is vital that we have those in leadership who are disciples committed to following Jesus Christ. If not, their decisions will be made for a variety of reasons, but not to be in service to Christ. If we have any hope of winning this war for the souls of persons we must do all in our ability to ensure that first-rate leaders are at the head of the pack, ready and able to lead an army of disciples. Way too many churches have a commander in chief (pastor) who knows what the mission needs to be, but does not have the officers (board or chairs) to lead others in the carrying out of that mission.

A church that does not have a solid choir director is likely not to have a solid choir.

A church that does not have a committed Sunday school teacher is likely not to have quality education.

A church that does not have generous stewards as leaders is likely not to have a generous congregation.

Some years ago I was asked to do a study of a church that had a long history of very poor giving. This church seemed to have everything necessary to be a solid church. They had a gifted pastor. They had a beautiful building with ample room. They were in a growing community in a great location. What was wrong? As I studied them I found out that the pastor was denied any access to the church donor records. This forced him to guess on the discipleship faithfulness of his congregation. He tried to guess well. I, however, because of the study, got access to these records and what I found out was that of the fourteen members on the finance committee, only two were included in the top one hundred donors to the church. Several gave nothing at all. These were the persons who were charged with raising the budget to carry out the mission. Personally, they did not want to give, so they did not want the church to ask for much. As a result they exercised their leadership abilities to meet as low a standard as possible. I wrote all of this up in my report, got my check and received their thanks. Two weeks later the pastor called to tell me that the committee had decided to table the report and put it on the shelf to be reviewed at some later date. For lack of leaders this church was not going to move out on the front lines. Their commander in chief had spelled out what the mission ought to be, and he had done that well. However, the appointed generals and officers in the field would not carry out the mission because they themselves did not want to be a part of it.

If you want to win this war, you have to see that top leaders are in place first. This begins by having a covenant within the church that all leaders sign stating that, as a leader, they understand that they are to uphold the expectations of discipleship in such a way as to be an example to others. They will lead in worship, service, prayer, study, witness, and giving. These expectations will be spelled out and each is asked to sign before they become leaders. They may refuse and choose to continue to be a foot soldier, but if they wish to lead they have to be willing to exemplify leadership ability in the way they are committed to the mission. This is not always easy, but it is vital. There is a war on and right now we are losing for lack of good leaders.

Here is where laity can truly lead the way. The pastor (commander) can say that these are the traits the church needs in a leader, but he or she will not be heard like a layperson who stands and says it. "We must..." is so much better than "You must..." In the army this is where a general will often look to a top sergeant to go address the troops. That person is one of them.

Within the church I often say we need more leaders who have been to the Emmaus Road than to Wall Street. Way too often I have seen persons chosen to lead in generosity who understand money, but have no understanding of the mission of making disciples. They will lead a church to balance a budget but not to save a soul. They were chosen because they knew how to lead a bank or lead a company or be a great entrepreneur or for any number of reasons other than actually having a strong commitment to the ministry of Jesus. Let me be clear. We are in combat to win the world for Jesus, period. That is our mission. Anyone who does not understand that completely and is not totally dedicated to it will only be a drawback to fulfilling the mission. You are better off without them.

You Need the Army, Navy, and Air Force

In my first combat experience, the first casualty was the loss of a naval aviator. The first month of fighting was led by wave after wave of air force planes preparing the battlefield. Finally the army and marines mounted up and marched across the border to take and hold land, which led eventually to victory. Air, land, and sea were fully utilized to achieve the best result in the quickest amount of time. It may have been possible for just one branch of the service to have won this war, but it was not likely. It certainly would have been much more difficult, caused many more casualties, and taken a lot more time.

For the church to win in creating generous disciples to transform the world we must do a much better job of teaching persons how to give from more than just one pocket. In an overwhelming majority of churches all of the generosity emphasis is on giving from the earned income (annual) pocket. This is the same pocket we use for rent, groceries, and other weekly cash flow items. It is from where our offering-plate money is solicited. We totally ignore the availability of the capital and estate pockets. If we are going to go for victory we have to learn to utilize all three of the pockets available to us.

The first pocket is the annual fund or earned income. This is something we do fairly well. We pass a plate every seven days and give people an opportunity to give to the ongoing operations of the church. We can, in most cases, do it much better. We must create an atmosphere around the offering that makes giving an integral part of worship instead of having a feeling of it being "time out." Before every offering there should be a personal testimony about the impact that the church and its ministries have had on one's life. This testimony should be personal—not just some announcement that $1,000 was sent to help build a water well in Africa. It should not come from the pastor or liturgy leader, but from the individual who actually experienced the ministry or had the life experience. Taking one minute before every offering for such a witness will be the single biggest thing you can do to increase the amount given through the annual fund. In the beginning this will require a staff person or key volunteer to undertake the responsibility of getting the testimony lined up, but after about two months you should find that the testifiers will self-identify and easily fill up the future Sundays. Doing the testimony by video is preferred because of the ability to control the time and exactly what is said, and works just as well as having the testimony in person.

One of the sayings in the army is that they want to be so strong and dominant that no one would ever want to challenge them to the point that they have to fight. That is by far the preferred approach. Fighting is usually the sign that something failed elsewhere. The goal of your annual fund is to create a foundation of ministry that has such an impact that there is not a need for an annual fund drive. Having to have such a drive is an admission that the church has failed to make generous disciples. The vast majority of strong Protestant churches in America do not have annual fund campaigns. The people have a generosity culture and a strong sense of gratitude to God and they just give. However, as author Herb Mather says, "You don't shoot the horse till you have learned to drive the tractor."[2] Go ahead and have your annual pledge drive, but have it as your goal not to need it within three years.

The second pocket of giving is the capital pocket. This pocket is full of appreciated and accumulated assets like stocks, bonds, property, insurance, inheritances, and sudden liquidity events (like selling a business). We do not plan on using these assets to pay our rent or to buy groceries so we set them aside usually in some investment account and wait for a future opportunity to draw from it. It is from this pocket that charities frequently tap from for buildings or big dream projects that are not in their daily operating needs. Churches also seek gifts from this pocket, but they do it much too infrequently. Maybe once every ten or twenty years when a building is being considered or property is being bought will they have a "Capital Campaign" and seek such a gift. In the meantime, every college, hospital, and most major nonprofits are making opportunities available for such giving every day.

If someone inherits a lot of money from a mother or father and wants to donate a considerable amount in memory, they are not going to just sit around with that money for a decade to see if the church just might need it. No, they are going to be looking right away and the college or hospital will have an immediate need that can be discussed that very day. I cannot tell you the dozens, and perhaps hundreds, of times in my career that I went to visit a donor only to hear that they sure would like to give a major gift to the church but just last year they gave to _____ (*fill in the blank*).

Now do not think I am saying here that you have to always be building a building. If you do not need a building then you should not build one. What you should be conscious of every day is where God wants you to go that you have not gotten to yet. What ministry needs your attention? What wound needs to be healed? What mouth needs to be fed? What is happening in your community that you feel God would have you respond to, if only you had the resources? This is what you talk about and this is what you write about. You share a ministry dream. You share the "what if" with the congregation. You make sure that every day in your church you have a plan for one million dollars if someone walked in that day with the money and asked you what could be done with it.

Persons have the opportunity to give from the capital pocket at varying times in their life. You want to be sure that you are in line with a need when they begin to look for where to go with it.

The final pocket that everyone in every church has available is the planned giving or estate pocket. This is the pocket that generally becomes fully available at the time of a death. Every single person in every single church has the ability to give from this pocket. It is also the easiest pocket from which we can seek gifts. However, even though religion receives 32 percent of all charitable gifts and ranks number one in charitable giving categories, religion ranks fifth when it comes to bequest gifts. While it seems obvious that religion is the favorite charity for Americans, they are not choosing religion in their will or with trust arrangements. The reason is simple—we are not asking for those gifts.

In combat this would be like the army being in a significant battle and being bogged down in a foxhole. They enemy is shooting at you and you are shooting back. You cannot figure out how to turn the tide so you can move forward. Someone reminds you that right offshore is the navy and they have an aircraft carrier with eighty fighter jets. They have escorts of destroyers that possess dozens of cruise missiles and heavy guns. They have multiple helicopters and hundreds of marines but you decide not to call. Somehow, some way, you just want the army to do this all by themselves. You only want to win one way! That makes no sense and someone is liable to get court-martialed if that is a decision made.

If we are serious about winning in the combat for souls and lives we need to use estate or planned giving in every church. It is just sitting there waiting to go to work for the church. Endowments are marvelous instruments to do ministry that does not excite many within the church. Endowment income repairs broken HVAC systems. Endowment income replaces the roof. Endowment income tuck-points brick and paints sanctuaries. Endowments can care for the properties that house the ministries that are changing lives, while few people get excited over raising money for a roof. Raise money for a new nursery area and let endowment proceeds fix that roof.

Endowments can launch new ministries. How many times has someone come forth with a novel ministry idea that cannot get off the ground because no one can see how to fund it? Endowment proceeds can be seed money for one or two years to see if the ministry truly does meet a need.

Endowments can ensure that mission efforts or scholarship availability is there to be used forever and not just on a yearly budget basis. In short, endowment income can take a church way beyond where it is presently to meet the needs of people. But we have to ask for the pocket.

Every church should be reminding their members on a regular basis about putting the church in the will. It involves persons placing one sentence in a will document, and a will is a stewardship document. My preference has always been for a percentage statement to be in the will such as, "I wish 10 percent of my estate to go to First Church of Anytown, USA." That is all that is necessary. Without doing hardly any work at all, when a member dies the church gets a check from the estate that will provide for ministry needs forever.

Here is all you need to do:

1. Right now get an Endowment Policy and Gift Acceptance Policy in place to guide your receipt and management of gifts. These are easy to obtain and customize. Get it from your denominational foundation or from Horizonsstewardship.com.

2. Set up a plan on how you will communicate with the congregation that you hope they will consider the church in the will.

3. Contact your denomination foundation and arrange for a series of educational seminars to acquaint your people with planned giving opportunities.

4. Have a staff person or volunteer group set up to ensure that getting planned gifts is a priority item for the church going forward.

5. Answer the phone when an attorney calls to ask where to send the check.

When I was a soldier out in the sand of the Middle East, I would lie on my back at night with many of my fellow soldiers and watch the navy and air force planes fly overhead to do their work ahead of us. If always felt good to know that others were fighting for this mission too and that we were not alone.

This is how planned giving works. You do what you do, but you have requested the assistance of another pocket of giving that is working for you, even as you stand and watch. Put planned gifts to work for your mission today.

To me these are the big three pockets to help us win. We have to raise the level of expectations. We have to have the right and best leaders in place, and we must use all three pockets of giving available to us every day. Do this and the gospel wins.

Questions for Review

1. If your church set up high expectations and explained them to persons before they joined, do you think it would make a difference in your church over time? How do you feel that current members would respond to these expectations?

2. Do you think high expectations for a disciple are biblical?

3. In your church, do you regularly seek gifts from the annual, capital, and planned pockets? How could you improve?

4. Should those who are selected to lead have a different set of expectations than the followers? Should expectations of staff be different from lay leaders?

★ ★ ★

C h a p t e r   6

The Art of Spiritual Combat

The plans of the diligent lead surely to abundance,
but everyone who is hasty comes only to want.

Proverbs 21:5

I n the army one of the required reads of anyone destined to
be an officer and leader of persons is the classic book by Sun
Tzu called *The Art of War*. For more than a millennia it has
laid out fundamental principles on how to fight and, more importantly, how to win. Even today where there are nations and
factions and weapons unknown to Tzu, his basic principles are
still followed by many a soldier.

Within the art of spiritual combat where we are fighting for
the necessary resources to win our battles for the hearts and minds
of all persons, there are certain fundamental principles on how to
fight and win that need to be followed. The problem within the
church is that these principles are not known by many church
leaders and because of that not followed. Laypersons reading this
book need to know that very few pastors in America have any
training in fundraising (which every church does), running a

nonprofit (which a church is), motivating or recruiting volunteers (whom every church needs). So do not have expectations of leadership from your pastor in these areas. They are learning from this book at exactly the level many of you are.

When I went off for my basic officer training with the army, I was initially taught all the unique things about military service that I had never been exposed to. These were things that all soldiers understood and not particular to me, just to the army. Once they taught me the basics of that then they went to work on the particulars of what it was to be a chaplain. Upon graduation I was certified to go to combat, if necessary, and fully do my job.

When I went to seminary for my pastoral training I found out that I would get a lot of instruction specific to being a spiritual leader. I learned how to teach the Bible. I learned how to craft sermons. I learned how to think theologically. But absolutely no one taught me anything about money or how to raise it, manage it, or use it. I had never seen a balance sheet, yet I would instantly be placed in leadership in a finance meeting where questions would be asked about the balance sheet. I did not know anything about accounting management or even how to take up money, get it counted, deposited, and available for use. I certainly did not know anything about how to raise it.

This raised its head immediately when I arrived at my first assignment. Following the first Sunday, there were a series of meetings to get the new preacher up to speed on what had been going on and what they hoped the future would look like. One of those meetings was with the finance committee. When I got to the meeting I was informed that they had expanded their membership to include a recently elected building committee chairperson. After a few pleasantries the building chair was invited to take the floor. She began, "A couple of months before you arrived we had a church vote and voted to relocate to a new five-acre site on the edge of town. Additionally, we need to tear down that old house you are living in and either build a new parsonage or just give you an allowance to find your own. We are so glad you are here and look forward to your leadership to help us move forward."

I was trying hard not to let them see my horror. Relocate the church and build a new home? I was expected to be the leader of all this. I started by asking what seemed to be an obvious question, "How much money do we have for this?" The answer came back, "Twenty-five thousand dollars." Well I was no financial genius but I figured that was not going to be enough to do the entire job. "So what is the plan for the balance?" I asked. "That is what we were going to ask you. Again, we are so glad you are here." And they all looked at me.

I left that meeting to make numerous phone calls to denominational leaders seeking guidance and sadly got very little. I then went back to a collegiate fundraising executive and he gave me a number of pointers and shared some book titles and I devoured them all, trying to learn how to lead a church I was ill prepared to lead. In the end, we succeeded, but I think it was more because of the grace of this congregation than it was my leadership. Today we have the Horizons Academy of Faith and Money, which I created to attempt to educate clergy in the basics as I wish I had been trained. Hundreds of pastors have gone through it and I hope they found themselves more prepared for the battle than I was. If we are going to win this battle we must first learn the fundamentals.

People Give to People

This is a fundamental principle that most in the church have failed to grasp. The belief in the mission of the nonprofit may be the number one reason why people say they chose to give to something, but in most cases they also had some relationship with the person who was leading the mission. It was the degree of confidence they had in that person that would often make the difference in the degree of support. I would have much more confidence in committing to fight a battle if I felt Patton was in charge than if they told me Private Snuffy was leading. In a church this means that to win our fight for resources we have to have a leader (pastor) who through his or her building of relationships can establish confidence in persons to make commitments. When they do not have that confidence they may make a contribution, but not a commitment. Generally, the bigger commitment you seek necessitates the depth of relationship that is required.

I remember specifically in one church where we had a donor who was highly committed to a project with a six-figure gift. In fact, he had told me of his desire to make that gift very early on and even left the impression that it may grow as things progressed. The bishop chose to move the long-tenured pastor and bring in a younger person halfway through the campaign. The donor called me the day after the upcoming change was announced. "I am withholding my commitment," he said sternly. "Once I see if the new person is capable of leading this church in the right direction, I will consider it again." The project did not change. The need did not change. All that changed was the confidence level of the donor in the person who would now be in charge of the mission. As far as I know that gift never materialized.

Now, we can all sit back and chastise this particular donor for not being more blindly committed to the work of the church, but that will not help us win the battle. Not only is he not going to change but also neither are countless others who have numerous opportunities to do good and every day chose to donate to the place where they have relationships. We are better off learning to intentionally make sure those relationships are made.

Some are now reading this and saying that a pastor should not be building unique relationships with persons who have significant resources. Why not? Pastors develop unique relationships with all sorts of persons within the congregation depending upon their circumstances or talents. They have unique relationships with people who have gone through particular crises such as death or illness. They have unique relationships with those who go to men's club on Wednesday mornings. They have unique relationships with persons who are in the pastor's Bible study. They have unique relationships with those who joined the church under him or her and those who have been charter members. Having a unique relationship with persons who may have the capability of funding the mission the pastor is responsible for accomplishing just makes sense.

A key thing to remember is that *friendraising* is more important than *fundraising*. You should be ten times more intentional to make a friend than to get a gift. If you will put in the hours to cultivate a relationship, you will find that you only need to spend a few minutes to get a gift that can be used to advance the cause of Christ. I will share much more on this in an upcoming chapter on special forces and major gifts.

Chapter 6

Compelling Case

When I went to war in the Gulf it was made quite clear to us that we were going to help free the people of Kuwait from the dictatorial boot of Saddam Hussein and his army. They had brazenly invaded a sovereign nation and were torturing its people. We were to also help ensure that this madman did not gain control of much of the world's oil supply, which could cause an even wider and far more disastrous war. The case for us to be there was very clear and easy to understand.

Later, as most of you know, Americans were sent back to Iraq to rid the nation of WMD (weapons of mass destruction). None were found. We did get rid of Saddam but after that the case became very fuzzy and anti-war sentiment began to grow. People did not understand why we were there. Attempts to make the case faltered as time went on and results were not more evident. It has continued to be a problem to this day.

For your church to win the war against money and stuff you are going to have to make a "compelling" case. This is a case that begins with God calling us to do and be _____. This is a case that is easy to understand and is backed up with facts and hope. Your case must spell out how contributing to the church will change lives and make the world the place that God intended it to be. Your case cannot be that you need to raise a certain amount to fund the budget. No one cares about a budget. People care about children, the youth, the sick, the environment, the lost, the hurting, and the neglected. They care about whether they are on God's side or not. How is their money going to alleviate pain and suffering and bring help and hope? Oh, persons will give something out of obligation to an organization or family church but they will not make a commitment.

As you go about trying to raise the level of generosity, you are going to have to help persons see that being generous to you is the best way they can give to change the world. Imagine what will happen if you stand before them and can only say, "Last year we lost twenty-four more members than we brought in. We went from four children's classes to two. We did not baptize anyone. We have been unable to meet all our mission obligations due to the repairs needed on the boiler and our youth pastor will be going part-time. So we sure hope you will help fund the 10 percent budget increase so we can get back on track." You will fail!

I suggest you do what the army does. Write out your case on a single piece of paper and study it. If it is not compelling to you as to why this deserves support then go back to work on it until it is compelling. You need your army to want to volunteer to serve, not have to be drafted.

People Need to Give

People need to be generous not because you need money, but because their life depends upon it. This is fundamental to fundraising and growing generosity. If the emphasis is on the church getting versus the donor giving then you have lost the war before it starts.

If you will notice, there are two different types of ads used by the military branches. One emphasizes service and commitment and honor and the value of that to one's life. The other ad emphasizes how you can get your college paid for, get retirement in twenty years, and have great health insurance.

The church generally goes for the latter type of advertising when we talk about generosity. We tell people that they can name buildings after themselves or get other special recognition or just "be somebody." The greater emphasis should be placed on the value to their lives in discovering that greed and money do not bring satisfaction. It does not help you raise a quality family. It does not bring happiness. It does not secure an abundant life. It is fool's gold. Generosity builds character. It serves others. It lifts others up. As you lose your life, you gain life. The emphasis is on others, which strangely enough is the best thing for the self. You must help your members understand the difference with what you preach and teach.

I know a man who is miserable. He is now in an assisted living center and stays mostly off by himself. He is actually healthier than most of the persons at the center and quite capable of contributing to the betterment of their lives, but he stays mostly in his room and complains. One day I was talking to him and trying to lift up the plight of others in his own family. As I shared about this one and that, he interrupted me with, "But I am worried about ME!"

If your program on generosity focuses mostly on how it helps "the church," "the members," or "the donor," then it will fail. If, however, you can get your people to understand that the best thing they can do to enrich themselves is to give to others and get their focus to be outward versus inward, then you will have a generosity program of strength and power that can win battles and change lives.

Remember what you are involved in is spiritual combat. If you keep your focus on the spiritual need to be generous, the spiritual power of being generous, and the spiritual uplift of being generous, then you are likely to win. If it ever shifts to being about material combat and about money, you lose!

Questions for Review

1. How good is your program of intentionally building relationships with persons who can fund your mission?

2. Can you make a compelling case for people to want to give to you? Why does God want you to succeed in securing funds for your church?

3. What is the impact you have on your community? What would be the consequences of your going out of business tomorrow?

4. Do you seek money from persons because you need the money, or is it to help them grow in spiritual generosity?

5. What does it mean when someone says, "The church is a business and must run like one"?

6. Is your program of growing generosity spiritually driven or materially driven?

★ ★ ★

Chapter 7

A Battle Plan

Then Jesus told his disciples, "If any want to become my
followers, let them deny themselves and take up their cross and
follow me. For those who want to save their life will lose it,
and those who lose their life for my sake will find it. For
what does it profit them if they gain the whole world
but forfeit their life?"

Matthew 16:24-26

For weeks on end the soldiers of my unit had been preparing for something, but we were not exactly sure what. We had been told that we should expect to fight, so our tanks practiced various maneuvers and our soldiers did target practice. Our medical people prepared packets for the expected casualties and reviewed triage procedures. I had to write up a plan for spiritual care of our troops and how a half dozen units scattered over many miles would be cared for by a single chaplain and an assistant. Our logistics personnel had various contingencies for supplying food, bullets, blankets, armored vests, and other necessary items. All was occurring in somewhat of a vacuum. Then one day the commander called us all together and said that the battle plan had come down and we were to take our various pieces and weave them into a common operation that would lead to victory. We were seeking to win a war and free a nation from an oppressive occupier and we now had a plan.

If we as the church expect to win the war against secular society that glorifies getting over giving, and elevates greed over generosity, we will need a battle plan. The stakes are too high to go forward with each area of the church just performing in a vacuum without any understanding of how each piece is going to be used to save the souls of lost misguided persons. What does it profit God's kingdom if you have a great musical production but souls see it no differently than a nice night at the symphony? What good does it do in the overall battle for souls if you have a bigger youth attendance but only because you have a nicer gym than the church down the street? We are in a war and the objective is to bring persons into a realization that a relationship with Jesus Christ that leads to a generous life is the way to a victorious life, leading to eternal life.

A year-round plan for generosity development is our battle plan. This plan should be constructed a year in advance. This means that in January you are preparing the generosity plan that would begin in January of the following year, while at the same time executing the battle plan that has been in place for the previous twelve months. Deciding to do something about generosity development in July that you will execute in October is a sure way to fail. Just look at the history of doing such over the last fifty years. That is how long most churches have been following such a model to grow generosity. How's that been working for you? Remember the objective is not just to get some money (win a skirmish) but to win a war. We are not in this just to say we held onto a hill and maintained status quo. We are in this fight to save souls through a complete reversal of common thinking about faith and money. If you truly care about these souls then you want to fully defeat the enemy of greed and consumption and that will take a complete battle plan. It is your choice.

The Plan for Complete Victory

This Generosity Battle Plan was initially created by Joe Park, the managing partner at Horizons Stewardship, and presented to several hundred clergy at the Horizons Academy on Faith and Money.[1] I have adapted and elaborated on much of it, but Joe deserves credit for what has already proven to be a winning plan.

The plan is divided up around seasons of ministry in the life of most churches. You should work with your church calendar and actually date various pieces as closely as possible, however, versus just saying, "We will do this around the first of the year or during Lent." D-Day did not occur sometime in the summer but on June 6 because in the course of the war that day fit the best with all other concurrent events.

New Year

This is the absolute best time to launch personal finance instruction with classes and sermons. Persons are looking at all sorts of lifestyle changes as they start the new year, from diet to exercise programs to work habits. They are open to hearing messages around how God would have them shape their financial life.

Financial Peace University is the most widely used personal finance program in the Christian church.[2] It is excellent but not necessarily that much better than several others that are offered.

The reason that I recommend it first is because of the awareness of Dave Ramsey, persons are far more likely to sign up and participate. You will need to do a lot of publicity initially if your church has not used the program before. There should be testimony in worship with anyone who has gone through it. You will need informational brochures and posters around the church. The pastor or a staff person may want to go into the young adult Sunday school classes and make a personal invitation. There is a cost associated with the course and an older member may accept an invitation to gift the program to a certain number of young couples.

I will never forget the sermon I preached early on in my ministry on giving, and upon exiting the sanctuary I saw a young man quietly sobbing in the pew. When I went and inquired as to what the problem was he poured out his heart about how he so wanted to be generous and faithful with his gifts. He believed everything I was saying was correct and righteous, but in his current financial mess he could not see how to ever get there. In his eyes, I had just preached a sermon on sin without sharing with him how to get out of sin. He was trapped and felt hopeless. I felt terrible. Begin your year by sharing with your people that for all who believe that being generous is God's way of life you have a pathway to help them find hope and new life. You should have a lot of soldiers sign up. Once your first class goes well then the next will be much easier because you will have a dozen testifiers to the life-change that they have experienced.

Sermon Series

January is the best time to preach about becoming a generous person in the new year. Here is where you will want to lay out the life-giving power of generosity and the threat to our faith of greed and consumption. These sermons should center on developing a generous life and becoming a contributor to the vision of the church to truly be God's vehicle in the new year. You should carefully avoid any suggestion that the end-all is the acquisition of money or that the series is about meeting a manmade budget. At the first hint of these themes those who are listening with hungry hearts will shut you out and may never engage again.

My preference for the series is that it be three or four weeks long. There are numerous books available that you can use for material. Andy Stanley's *Fields of Gold* has seven chapters that can easily be worked into a good four-week series. Herb Miller's *Money Is Everything* has been out of print for some time but copies are around and it not only has six great chapters but also some wonderful illustrations. Randy Alcorn's *Treasure Principle* has some controversial sections but is very useful. I also recommend Mike Slaughter and Karen Perry Smith's *Christian Wallet*, Adam Hamilton's *Enough*, and of course, Henri Nouwen's the *Spirituality of Fundraising*.[3] If you cannot get a good sermon series from these then you may need to look for another kind of work.

Thanking People from the Start

The church is absolutely the worst institution at taking its donors and volunteers for granted. We seldom send thank-you notes and put on an air of arrogance when humility is far more called for. I have long admired the famous picture of General Eisenhower standing among the paratroopers of the 101st Airborne, the soldiers who would be the first to land on D-Day.[4] He was thanking them. This five-star general supreme commander was among the troops just to say thanks when all he had to do was order them to jump. They led the Allies to victory. If we are to go on to victory, our pastors need to do a lot more saying thanks to our soldiers. It strengthens for the battle in surprising ways.

Beginning with the very first Sunday of the year, the senior pastor should send a thank-you letter to everyone who makes a gift along with a small devotional guide gift (an inexpensive paperback is fine) saying thank you for giving to the church. This is then repeated throughout the year every time someone makes his or her first gift. Your letter should not only say thanks but also contain a brief word on generosity as a mark of a disciple and how it leads to abundant living. If the first-time donor for the year is a first-time donor EVER then a different and deeper letter can be sent along with either the devotional guide or even one of the books I mentioned earlier with an inscription from the senior pastor.

Do you have to take time to do this? Of course not, but it sure will help your disciples fight harder for victory than if you just take their gift for granted. It is your choice. Ike did not have to visit the docks either, but he did.

Planned Giving Promotion Starts

Be sure that you have your schedule set for quarterly planned giving and estate giving seminars to begin. February is a good month to get these underway. You should contact your denominational foundation and ask for their assistance with speakers, brochures, and promotional ideas. It is extremely important that you begin these early and consistently continue throughout the year.

Lent to Pentecost

This is a marvelous time in the life of the church. Worship is often amped up to its highest with services around Ash Wednesday, Palm Sunday, Good Friday, Easter, and Pentecost. This is the time when we celebrate the grace that forgives our sins with ashes on our foreheads. We look at Jesus's decision to go to Jerusalem knowing full well the sacrifice that would entail and the awful day when he suffered and died for us "while we were yet sinners." We sing "Hallelujah" that he rose from the grave to lay before us his plan for our redeemed lives that exploded on Pentecost with the power of the Holy Spirit. The themes are all around us in countless ways to explore discipleship and stewardship week after week. What does it mean to make a sacrificial decision? What have we ever sacrificed? Why do we dislike that word? What is the best response to new life offered in the Resurrection? Is there anything that keeps us from seeing Jesus in our midst today? Are we confident in the power of the Holy Spirit or the power of stuff to be our ultimate deliverer?

I am not advocating that you repeat the direct themes of faith and money throughout the Lent and Easter seasons, but to be mindful that it is money and stuff that is keeping most of the congregation from experiencing the true joys of new life. It should be lifted up in and around other preaching themes.

This is also the season that you should consider a tithing challenge. Beginning with the first Sunday of Lent and going to Pentecost Sunday challenge your congregation for these ninety days to give 10 percent of their income to the church in gratitude for the gift you are celebrating in a risen Christ and the Holy Spirit. Have them sign up so you can publicize how many are actually going to take the challenge. Promise them that just as Christ did you will let them go right back to their old life after the ninety days, if they are not convinced the new life exemplified in the tithe has been worth it.

The week after Pentecost send a note out to all the ones who accepted the challenge and see who is going to continue and who is choosing to go back to their previous pattern of generosity. For those continuing, consider having a few of them testify over the next several Sundays about what the experience has been like and why they are going to continue.

Your second planned giving seminar should happen during this time, as well.

Summer

This is a difficult time in most churches because so many families are sporadic in their attendance. It is a very good time to shift your focus to more one-on-one. Plan on going to lunch with someone once a week solely to learn about how and why they give. Review your donor list and certainly take note of the top ten to twenty families who probably make up a very significant portion of your revenue, but also look for the widow who is giving her coins.

With the high-donor families you will want to listen to what is in their heart and why they give as they do. Why have they chosen the church over so many other opportunities they might have? What guides their giving decisions? What are their highest hopes for the church that they just might help fund if such became a possibility? Your goals in these lunches are to LISTEN and to express THANKS. You do not want to solicit or be seen as having an agenda of wanting something from them.

In your meeting with "the widow" or "the widower," the conversation again centers on thanks, but you really want to probe into what her or his motivation is to give so generously. Dig deeply here to get at the root of what probably is a solid spiritual foundation around generosity. This is a person who may write an article for you to distribute or be willing to share a testimony on a Sunday morning that would be a great blessing to the congregation.

Summer is a good time for a staff retreat as all can get on the same page moving into the busy fall season. Setting a date early in the year will allow staff to plan their own vacations around the retreat. This is also a good time for you to have a conversation with staff members about their own discipleship witness. You MUST have high expectations for them in all areas of discipleship including stewardship. You will find that some will not be very comfortable as leaders and feel that their particular work with children, youth, or music is gift enough. Others will have issues around spousal support of giving. Some may have debt issues. It is important for the senior pastor to be a pastor to the staff but you must also hold them accountable. While on several staffs in the army, I found numerous staff officers who had personal issues and concerns, but they were all reminded that they volunteered for the job and the job must be done to the highest standards anyway. If they wore the uniform they were just as subject to being deployed as anyone else, whether they had one child or ten children, whether their mom was sick or well, whether they were in college or not. If you accept the job, then you accept the responsibilities of leadership that go with it.

We could not win the battles if each was offered the chance to get special consideration. It should be no different in the spiritual battle we are in. We must have top leaders willing to lead the way in serving and giving. It is what the job is. Jesus laid out numerous disciple expectations throughout the Gospels, knowing that such commitment in all areas would be necessary for God's kingdom to win the fight ahead. Some accepted the challenge and put on the armor of Christ. Others walked away unwilling to live up to the challenge. Jesus never wavered.

One more planned giving seminar can be added for the summer because senior citizens are much more available than younger families during this time of the year.

Fall

Fall is when it all starts back up for most churches. There are new classes, sermon series, and a renewed push to finish strong on the year. The annual campaign is also seen as the big event of fall. I will make an assumption that many of you will be doing annual campaigns, but repeat what I have done many times. Annual campaigns are an admission that we have failed to make disciples. Unless your church is growing at a rate of 10 percent a year and needs a campaign to encourage spiritual discipline, there is just no reason why you should have to be reminding people every year that a disciple is called to be generous by inserting gimmicky boxes of materials into their worship services and homes. If we would begin by lifting up high expectations prior to people joining and teaching generosity throughout the year, people will be as faithful in their generosity as they are with other vows they have taken and do not have to be reminded of every fall.

However, I am going to assume that most of you just read this and said that is all well and good but you are going to do a campaign for annual pledges. I am not going to recommend any certain one, because it is very individualized by the type of church you are, but I will share some components that should be a part of any:

1. Your emphasis should be on ministry and not money. DO NOT DISTRIBUTE A LINE ITEM BUDGET! A line item budget says nothing about ministry. The budget you share must be a missional or narrative budget where every dollar is divided up into ministry areas. Examples of these budgets are in previous books I have written. These budgets can have great impact on persons' responses. They give to change lives and not to balance budgets. Missional budgets share clearly how that is being done.

2. A significant percentage of your budget comes from five to ten families. These families must be visited with on a one-to-one basis. The pastor should do it and a specific "ask" must be made of each family. Just saying "I hope you will help" will not work!

3. Correspondence with all other families must be targeted. Do not send the same letter to all. To your top people the emphasis of the letter is "Thanks." To your consistent givers it is growth. To the occasional giver it is to be more consistent. To the non-donor it is to consider $5.00 a week. Again, example letters are in other books I have written.

4. A set Sunday should be determined when pledges will be asked for of the general congregation. Major donor gifts should already have been announced. Go two weeks after this commitment Sunday and declare the campaign over. Do not drag it on for weeks and weeks. Have a termination date.

5. When you do your accounting be sure and count all active donors who may not have turned in a card. They almost certainly will.

6. Do not prepare your budget from the pledges. Pledges are just to assist people with their own spiritual discipline. Prepare your budget from the income you expect in the current year.

Have your fourth and final planned giving seminar during this time, being sure to include the question on the annual pledge card, "Would you like for someone to contact you regarding a planned or estate gift to the church? Check here."

End of the Year

Thanksgiving and Christmas time! This is the time frame when the enemy plans numerous attacks with their consumption weapons to try hard to disrupt any attempt at focusing us on generosity. One would think that the very word *Thanksgiving* would help all of us think about giving thanks with how we give, but the opposition forces have found a weak link in our defenses with a massive emphasis on eating until almost ill, and then throwing away millions of pounds of food. Under the guise of giving thanks we have family feuds, recipe arguments, and political prayers. Most persons are absolutely worn out by the entire experience and the idea of growing as a more generous person moves further and further away from their consciousness. As persons scrub the roasting pan violently to remove dried turkey drippings, all they are thankful for is that the day is over! Battle lost!

This is then followed by Christmas with one commercial after another espousing the virtue of wearing a certain perfume, brand-name shirt, or $250.00 sneaker. How could anyone be happy at Christmas unless his or her home has a more elaborate décor than the others in the neighborhood? Our highest goal is to be sure that we spend and spend and spend so that every child and grandchild has an equal amount of gifts and that our friends get something from us that is more expensive than what they will give us. My friend and colleague Mike Slaughter wrote a great book several years ago called *Christmas Is Not Your Birthday* in an attempt to remind persons that this season is about God's generosity and we celebrate it by being generous as he is generous—not throwing elaborate parties and running up mounds of debt.[5] His book pushed back the forces of evil for a short while, but again this Christmas season they will regroup and attack us again.

Preaching

All this being said, one of the top weapons we have is the pulpit. The messages must not be just on how good God is to send his Son and to bestow so many blessings upon us, but what our responsibility is in response to such grace. Too many sermons around Thanksgiving talk about how thankful we should all feel with our fine homes, cars, 401(k)s, and fancy Sunday clothes. So what? How do Christians respond to grace? They become graceful. This is the time to preach a message of costly grace. God did not give his grace to us that we could just take it and do as we pleased. He bestowed his grace that we would then do likewise to those not so blessed. We are blessed to be a blessing.

The Advent season must be a time when the extreme generosity of God is laid before the congregation just as the nativity scene with the baby is put on display. This was an undeserved gift sent to us that we might have life and have it abundantly.

Jesus did not come that we might have a Lexus and drive it glowingly. He did not come that we might wrap the skins of numerous minks around our shoulders so that others would know that we can afford such a coat. He did not come that we might give our children and grandchildren so many gifts that some are never used and many quickly forgotten. This is a time for bold preaching on generosity as seen in the gift of Christ to the world. One of the saddest occurrences in this war for the soul of humankind is that two of the most special "giving days" of the year have been totally turned upside-down with the cannon barrels turned toward the church. Instead of making up great ground on these very holy days, we find ourselves in massive retreat. How can we reverse the tide of battle other than with more powerful preaching?

Wish List for the Church

This is an excellent time to publish a wish list of items needed by the church so that you can be in more effective ministry. It could be chairs for the children's choir area or a new van for senior citizens. Let persons know what concrete things they may want to do. With each passing day donors are showing us that they like the idea of designated giving. Give them the chance.

Giving Equal to What They Are Spending

This idea from Slaughter's book encourages families to calculate what they will be spending over the Christmas season and to spend an equal amount on a particular mission effort. It is catching on in many churches and has become habit in several.

Informing Persons of Their Gifts to Date

Send targeted letters or emails to all your families letting them know what the church has done to change lives in the past year and what their contribution is to date. Even if it is zero, they should get a letter and a hope message that they can still be a part of the transformations happening at the church. This mailing should go out the week after Thanksgiving so as to give persons several weeks to catch up their giving, if they have fallen behind.

Annual Legacy Dinner

The week prior to Thanksgiving is a great time to host a dinner thanking all those who have informed the church that they have included the church in a will or trust. It should be a fun evening with music and a special speaker but also include a word on the status of the church's endowment along with how it has been used to benefit the ministry and mission of the church in the past year. Always encourage legacy society members to invite a guest to the dinner. This is a good way to recruit additional members.

Christmas Eve

This service is known to be the highest attended service of the year in the Christian church. Take advantage of this fact by making the service one of the best in music and word. The offering for the service should feature a special video presentation of how it will be used to serve those outside the church. You can announce that any persons wishing to give as a part of the annual church gift need to so mark their check. All unmarked gifts will go to missions. You will have numerous nonmembers in worship this evening and they are not very motivated to give to the church operations. They will, however, respond to giving to those away from the church and do so often in very generous ways.

Consistent Focus

As my army unit was shaping its battle plan with particular and special emphasis on certain things at certain times by certain people, our commanders were fully aware of numerous necessities that could not be overlooked every day. The soldiers had to be fed and fresh water had to be made available. Fuel had to be in ample supply for us to maneuver and weapons had to be cleaned and operational. Someone had to see that daily sanitation was covered and that provisions were made for personal hygiene. Neglecting any of these could cause us to lose the battle once the word came down that it was time to fight.

Likewise in the church. If we are going to combat the enemy of consumption and greed and grow generous disciples there are certain things that must be done regularly in every situation.

1. Every worship service must have a testimony of changing lives prior to the collection of the offering.

2. Each week thank-you letters must be written to donors and others who have chosen to give of themselves in some way to the work of the church. I recommend five to ten a week.

3. Each week the senior pastor receives an updated donor record to review and study to discern how he or she should prioritize time in the mission of creating generous disciples.

4. Every month in a large church (350-plus in worship), and every quarter in smaller ones, a donor letter and statement should go out. Always include a ministry story with the donor statement and, where possible, make it personal.

5. Be sure your church is giving all persons an opportunity to give as he or she is comfortable. Writing checks is archaic and unfamiliar to many young families. Be sure you make online giving, QR code giving, ACH, kiosk giving, and any other form of e-giving possible as you can. No church is too small to invest in this basic necessity.

6. Every week as you plan for how to best use the sermon, hymns, and anthems, pay attention that the offering does not come across as an afterthought. How can you be certain that it is lifted up to feel a full and important part of our living out our calling to be a generous disciple?

I did not put a capital campaign in this year-round generosity plan, but it is important that it be an annual discussion within the church. Persons have capital gifts they can make every year that you will not get if they are not sought. I am going to address this in the last chapter of the book in more detail, but it needed lifting up here so that it does not become a part of the battle that you only consider every ten years or so.

Questions for Review

1. How can you best prepare a year-round generosity plan for your church? Do you think it would make a difference?

2. What part of the plan presented here seems the most realistic for you? Most unrealistic?

3. Do you believe that if you had such a plan ongoing that you could eventually do away with the annual campaign drive?

4. I mention the need to thank people with notes and letters on a regular basis. When can this get started in your church and who should do it?

★ ★ ★

C h a p t e r   8

Special Forces

*The plans of the diligent lead surely to abundance, but every-
one who is hasty comes only to want.*

Proverbs 21:5

*Jesus said to him, "If you wish to be made perfect, go, sell
your possessions and give the money to the poor, and you will
have treasure in heaven; then come and follow me." When the
young man heard this word, he went away grieving, for he
had many possessions.*

Matthew 19:21-22

O n my long flight back to the United States following the
Gulf War I found myself sitting beside a fellow army
captain. We struck up a conversation about home and
family and good food. All the expected things one would expect
two deployed soldiers would discuss. I mentioned to him that I
had served with First Armor and a bit of what it was like to be
with all those tanks rolling across the desert. He shared that he
had been on the same ground about a month ahead of me, living
in a hole and capturing the intelligence we would need for the

big ground offensive. He was an Army Special Forces operator. He went into enemy territory, not with all the comforts of heavy armor and thousands of additional soldiers. He went ahead of us with only what he could carry and three other soldiers. What they did in advance is what allowed us to succeed weeks later. We both had on the same uniform, but we had very different responsibilities.

In fighting the war against the "have it all" society the church must have those persons who will go before others and take the lead. They must not only show that they have the capacity to lead but also the will to lead. I talked to my new friend about his training and he shared that showing one has the physical tools to withstand grueling conditions is what is tested first. He noted that most of those who test pass this initial level. However, the next phase tests the will to succeed. It is much more mental than physical. Here is where 70 percent drop out or are removed. Part of our job as church leaders is to identify and enlist these church persons who have not only the capacity to lead (ability to give significant gifts) but also more importantly the will (commitment to the mission) to do so.

Finding Your Special Forces

It has become in vogue in recent years to place a great deal of emphasis on doing data searches. There is an enormous amount of personal information on the internet about most of us. Quite often you can find out what persons' salaries are, real estate holdings, stock investments, company positions, and a laundry list of information that will give you an idea of what a person's wealth is. How else do you think *Forbes* comes up with its list of the richest persons in the world? This sort of computer searching is not totally unhelpful, but it has been given far too much weight. By just spending a little bit of time, using some common sense, and buying a couple of lunches you can discover things far more valuable than what the internet will tell you.

Major Gift Fundraising Is All about Relationships

On page 1 of chapter 1 of any fundraising primer will be "People Give to People." Major donors in particular are very sensitive to exactly who will be managing any charitable investment they choose to make. They are keenly aware that just money by itself makes little difference, but money in the right hands can change the world. Major donors want to know who is going to be seeing that what they want actually occurs. This is why almost all nonprofits use their CEO as the chief fundraiser for their organization. The CEO has more singular power than anyone else to see that a certain vision is accomplished or not. A major donor needs to have a relationship with this person to the degree that such confidence is established. This is relationship building.

What you are asking someone to do is go before all others. They do not yet have confidence that a goal or project will be fulfilled because little has been done at this point. All they have is a relationship with someone that they trust will get it done. This takes time and simply cannot and should not be rushed. *Friend-raising* trumps *fundraising* every time. If you have done a good job of plowing the field, planting the seed, weeding out the grass, watering the ground, and fertilizing the soil, then the harvest months later will be easy. If, however, you try and rush and skip some of these steps your harvest will be minimal at best. You must plow and water before you pick.

I visited one time with a very active church member. He had recently made two gifts. One was to his church and the other was to his college. The one to the college was twenty times the size of the one to the church. I sat in his living room and asked him how he had come to the conclusion to distribute his wealth as he had.

Immediately, he began to share with me the relationship he had developed with the president of the college. He commented that he personally had come to see him six to seven times over the last year. In those visits they had discussed wealth and how it can be a blessing and a curse. They discussed what success was like and how it compared to significance. They talked about the mission of the college and the president's vision going forward. Eventually the president asked this man if he and his wife would consider funding a significant portion of that vision and the gift was made.

In talking with this donor I asked him how many pastors he had had over the forty years he had attended his church. He told me, after counting up, that it was seven. I then asked him how many of his pastors had ever engaged with him around the issue of wealth. Had any sought to establish the sort of trusting relationship that the president had and even ventured into discussions around money? Very quickly he said, "No, but that was okay. You know that pastors do not like to talk about money."

Now pastors need relationships with numerous persons within their congregations who struggle with issues of all sorts from addictions to marriage to sickness and death. These often come easy. Building a relationship with persons who struggle with how a disciple is to manage his or her money is often overlooked.

My experience is that persons of wealth want help and spiritual counsel to determine the right thing to do. This takes time and, like hoeing the ground of weeds, may not show immediate fruit. But the potential for a great harvest is there if done right.

So where do you start as you make your plan to cultivate your special forces team? You have to identify who the best candidates might be. The best place to begin is to take the most up-to-date donor list and explore who is giving now. It is a given that those who are presently giving are the most likely to give in the future. Do not just look at who the top ten may be, but explore way down your list to see what you can learn. Someone may not be in the top ten, but they are in the top fifty and they just joined the church six months prior. Someone may not be in the top ten, but they have been consistent donors and faithful church members and you know they are selling a large tract of land. Someone may not be in the top ten but they are excellent donors with a modest income and lifestyle. They also teach Sunday school and are highly respected. All of these persons should be on your radar as potential persons who would be willing to step out early and lead the way to challenge others.

When you are looking over these donor records a myriad of questions should be going through your mind. How much have they given this year and in years past? Has it been consistent or sporadic? Do they give often or just once a year? Do they give just to the operating budget or have they shown leadership with capital campaigns or mission fundraisers? If they made a large gift before, why did they do it? Was it out of love for the church or did they just get an inheritance that will not be repeated?

In trying to identify a major donor you look for what kind of job they have, car they drive, house they live in, or family they come from. You see what you can learn about any gifts they may have made to others. These gifts are often in the paper or made public. All of this information will give you an idea of what the capacity of the donor might be. If you determine that they surely have capacity then you just have to fill in the blank on "the will to give" and you have the two things you need.

Determining will is fun. You certainly see "will" if they are consistent, faithful donors presently. However you will want to go further. Here is where going to lunch is a great idea. This lunch is a fishing expedition. You want to know why they give. How do they determine what is right to give? What is their story in coming to the church and coming to faith in Christ? What do they have a real passion for? If they could do anything in the church right now to make it better what would that be? You are putting numerous hooks into the water asking one probing question after another as you learn about this person and whether he or she could be a part of your special forces.

Eventually You Ask

Henri Nouwen said,

Once we are prayerfully committed to placing our whole trust in God and have become clear that we are concerned only for the kingdom; once we have learned to love the rich for who they are and rather than what they have; and once we believe that we have something of great value to give them, then we will have no trouble at all in asking someone for a large sum of money. We are free to ask for whatever we need with the confidence that we will get it.[1]

Once you have spent time cultivating and learning all you can about the potential major donor, you plan on making your ask. Several things come into play when you prepare to make an Ask.

Timing—You need to give serious thought to when is the best time to make the Ask. When in their lives does it seem best? Are they presently distracted by some other matter and it would be difficult for them to focus on a major giving decision? Have they recently sold a large piece of property, come into an inheritance, sold a business? These events are what I call liquidity events. Cash has suddenly appeared and decisions are actively being made on what to do with it. You do not want to wait long to get in line after a liquidity event. Do you need to see them morning, noon, or night? All these things should be thought through.

The Setting—An Ask can be made at a home, office, restaurant, or at the church. You need to decide with each person where the best place is. I prefer the most private place I can find where the donor will feel the most comfortable. For me, that means their office or home usually works best. Of these two it may matter as to whether the spouse is included. You always want to invite the spouse to such a meeting and let the couple decide who will be present. Never intentionally leave one out.

Who—It must be determined who should make the Ask. Remember an Ask is all about relationship. Most often in the church that is the pastor but not always. Sometimes it is realized that a fellow layperson is in a much better position by virtue of a relationship as well as awareness of the need to make the Ask. Occasionally a layperson will be accompanied by the pastor, but I hesitate to do this so as not to outnumber the donor and cause an uncomfortable situation.

Passion—An Ask always begins with the pastor or layperson sharing his or her passion for the project. This project should be well known to the potential donor and they should have few, if any, questions because the two of you have dealt with these over the months of cultivation. You just want to remind the donor you are personally invested and enthusiastic about what his or her possible investment will mean in the life of the church. Be fully prepared to share your own commitment if he or she inquires. Your gift does not have to be as large as his or hers, but it does have to appear to be proportional to what you are asking them to do.

The Number—After about five to six minutes you need to place a number in front of the potential donor. My words usually are, "I am hoping you will consider a gift of _____ (to make this a reality or lead others or inspire the congregation)." It is then important to shut up. Just stop talking and wait for his or her answer.

The Answer—You will get a yes. If so, you thank the donor profusely, wind up your visit, and go immediately and write him or her a thank-you note with reference to the gift to be sure all are on the same page.

You will get a maybe. The donor wants to consult with a spouse or advisor or think about it for a while. This is always appropriate. Your response is appreciation and gratitude for his or her consideration. Be certain to establish a set time when you will hear from him or her such as "in a week" or "by Sunday." This will keep you from wondering what is going on and it also gives you a legitimate reason to call if you have not heard by the agreed-upon time. Again, immediately go and write a thank-you note.

You will get a yes, but not that much. You may have asked for $100,000 but the donor said he or she cannot go that high.

I then ask at what level he or she would feel more comfortable. Upon getting an answer you thank the donor and immediately go write a thank-you note.

You will get a no. Perhaps you totally misjudged your interactions during cultivation or something occurred you were unaware of, but the answer is no. This really should never happen if you have done good cultivation. Generally, when this occurs cultivation was greatly short-circuited. But if you get a no, you thank him or her for giving you the opportunity to ask, and you again go write a graceful thank-you note.

It is not hard. In fact, once you have done an Ask once or twice you will find that it gets easier and easier. Remember, you will only get one of four answers. It is not that tough to prepare for four responses.

Because of the work of my Army Special Forces friend in gathering intelligence when it was time for all of us general soldiers to go to work, we found much smoother sailing. Neither of us would have succeeded without the other. It was vital for them to go ahead of us and the intelligence we got from them gave us much greater confidence that we could succeed. It was likewise important for us to use what they sent and build on that with the masses so that our mission would be accomplished.

Way too many churches think they will move forward in a fundraising effort by simply getting the army of the congregation to all move forward as one. Wouldn't that be nice? The fact is it does not work. Persons have to be led and they need confidence to follow. This is where major donors come into play. They have a particular blessing of wealth and will to give a congregation confidence and shine light on what seemed dark. When a congregation can hear that just a few have already stepped up to do so much, they become inspired to look deeper into what they might do because winning now seems like a possibility.

Do not even think about going to war against the forces of greed and money without having a special forces team ready to quietly and efficiently lead the way.

Questions for Review

1. Does your church allow full access to all donor records by the pastor? Why or why not? Why do you think your policy is the best way to serve God's kingdom?

2. In the past, has an awareness of leadership gifts been helpful to you or to a campaign in obtaining additional support?

3. Why do you think some persons in a church frown and gossip when they hear that the pastor is having lunch or visiting with persons of wealth when they do not do so when the pastor visits a nursing home?

4. Do you see Jesus having concern for the wealthy in society or just the poor?

5. Has an intentional major gift strategy ever been discussed by the leadership of your church?

★ ★ ★

Chapter   9

The Big Guns

*Who then will offer willingly, consecrating themselves to the
work of the Lord?... Then the people rejoiced because these had
given willingly, for with single mind they had offered freely to
the Lord. King David also rejoiced greatly.*

1 Chronicles 29:5-9

T he day had finally come and the orders came down for
my army unit to mount up and roll across the border
of Iraq. It was an amazing sight. For as far as I could
see right and left, front and back, were mighty M1A1 Abrams
tanks. Overhead we could see B-52 bombers, Apache helicopters,
and fighter jets. As we were about the get into formation for our
final instructions, the commander came over to me and offered
me a Beretta 9mm pistol and several clips of ammunition. As a
chaplain, I was to be a noncombatant and did not carry a weapon,
even though I always qualified with my guys on the range. I told
him politely that I was not authorized and he said, "All my chap-
lains in Vietnam carried a weapon and I just thought you would
be more comfortable with one." I replied, "Thank you, sir, but if
these Abrams and bombers and choppers cannot get the job done,

I seriously doubt that my little pistol will make much of a difference." He grinned and we rolled.

This occurrence sort of reminded me of the time in junior high when I and another friend were tasked to break up a gasoline pump island. These are the raised concrete islands that the gasoline pump sits on in front of a station. The pump had been removed, but the raised concrete island was still there. We had two sledgehammers and two picks. We started early in the morning pounding on the concrete. After an hour or so, one piece came loose. After another hour another small piece came loose. Same thing happened after another hour. At noon we were nearly spent and 90 percent of the island still stood strong. We sat down with a sandwich and an RC Cola and bemoaned our fate. Not long after we heard an engine fire up. From the corner of the station came a giant backhoe. That backhoe hit the island about three times and it busted to pieces. A chain was quickly wrapped around what was left and suddenly the island was gone. My friend and I were dumbfounded. We worked for four hours and made almost no headway. The backhoe worked for about four minutes and the job was complete. I asked the backhoe driver why he did not step in earlier and he said, "You never asked."

In the work of the church, if we want to win the war, we need to understand what tools are most needed and when they are needed. If my army unit needed to capture one soldier hiding in a hole, then my little pistol might have worked. If we had needed to remove one concrete post from a hole, then the sledgehammer and pick might have worked. However, the jobs at hand required much stronger tools if we were to succeed. In the church, when it comes to securing significant funds rapidly and growing generosity in the shortest possible time period, a capital campaign is the big gun that must be employed. Done correctly, a church can expect to receive multiples of its income and have an extraordinary impact upon its future and the spiritual health of the congregation. Done incorrectly, things can feel like you are pounding a concrete island for hours on end with little results to show for all the effort and a demoralized congregation.

Capital campaigns are built around the accumulated wealth of persons. These assets are not a part of the normal cash flow of a family. They are stocks, bonds, savings, inheritances, insurance policies, property, and so on. But they are all gifts from God to be used as God would have us do. Persons have these assets set aside and available if and when a particular demand arises. Often the particular demand is a charitable contribution for something the donor highly values and toward something the donor wants to make a significant impact. Most nonprofits market for these gifts every year. They always have a major need ready to go and make their potential donors aware of it, even if they are not considering doing it immediately. They do not want to miss out on the opportunity of the gift. Capital opportunities once missed are gone forever. The church has done a very poor job of keeping dreams and hopes in front of its donors. We have missed billions of dollars for our mission because a donor assumed the church had no particular need and used the capital gift at a hospital, college, or other charity. Every year we need to place something in front of our people that would take the church beyond what its annual spending can do to give donors the chance to consider using their capital pocket in this way.

Save your big guns for when they are really needed. Again, if I need to knock over one post then I probably do not need a backhoe. If I am going to break up an eight-foot concrete island,

I do. In the church, your measuring stick is your annual budget. If you are needing no more than your annual budget then you do not need a full-fledged capital campaign. It will be overkill and can even harm generosity. You could wear out your high-potential givers with little asks here and there until they no longer want to listen when you really need their firepower. This hurts the church and hurts these persons from experiencing how they could really make a huge difference. If you need an amount over your budget then a capital campaign may well be warranted.

The timing of your campaign is important. You want to strike when you have the highest opportunity to succeed. You will need good buy-in from the congregation. You will need a solid leadership team in place, and you should never proceed without having a professional feasibility study completed. Once these things are in place you can commence with a three- to five-month-long campaign. Capital campaigns do not and should not happen quickly. Since you need a number of months to succeed you must be careful with where Christmas, Easter, spring break, and other things occur that will rightly distract the focus of the congregation. Summer is a very poor time to try and get the focus of a congregation except in some places that have a large influx of population during the summer months. Rule of thumb—have a plan in place nine to twelve months out from where you want your capital campaign to start.

The biggest question you must answer for your people is, "Why does God want us to do this?" Remember, God is who we serve and that is whose gifts we will be giving. Does God want this church and these families to use his resources in this way? If you cannot answer this then go back to square one until you can. It should never be about getting money for the church. It is always about how we can serve God better. It is about our need to be a part of his plan to redeem the world and transform lives. Every congregational meeting and every discussion about the project or campaign should begin with a reminder of what the ultimate mission is.

Let me say this about mission. Often persons will say that they are going to have a capital campaign and want to add a 10 percent add-on for mission. They will say, "Since we are doing so much for ourselves we thought we should do something for others." Stop! If your campaign is not 100 percent about mission and serving others then do not do it. There should not be some sort of mission add-on. It should all be mission. Is a new sanctuary being built so that persons who have not heard the Word might hear it? Is a new educational complex not about teaching those about Jesus who do not know him? Is a new boiler not being installed so that people may find warmth in which to grow in Christ? If you think what you are doing is selfish, then do not do it!

One of the earliest decisions you will make is whether you should have outside professional counsel. Congregations will have big fuss-fights over this expenditure even though it generally amounts to no more that 2–3 percent of all the funds they will raise. For no more than this, why would it not make sense to have a professional on board versus risking such a huge effort to persons who have little or no experience in running such? I played football in junior high. I have been a season ticket holder for a major college team for decades. I watch dozens of games a year on television. I know football, but do you want me coaching your team in the Super Bowl? I know the rules. I could call plays, but just as soon as we fell behind or found adversity could I still lead a team in mutiny as well as Bill Belichick? No way, he has a great track record of success. He is a proven leader. He will be listened to and can unify the team. He can inspire confidence and get the most out of his players. I would fold at the first fumble!

You will need counsel if you truly want to win the war to make generous disciples. Not having it is a fool's errand that could cause a defeat your church may never get over.

You must have counsel if:

- You want to raise twice the amount you would raise otherwise. Professional help consistently outperforms self-run campaigns nearly two to one.

- You want your pastor to be able to focus on his or her strengths. In my twenty-five years of running Horizons, I have yet to find one pastor who felt that raising money was a great strength. It certainly was not why he or she entered into ministry. If your church tries to go it alone, your pastor will take energy from a strength (preaching, teaching, counseling, and caring) and be forced to spend energy on running an effort he or she has no experience in. When that happens the church suffers all around.

- You want your church to remain unified. If you do not have counsel on board to speak authoritatively to a strategy then you will quite often find various congregation members in conflict over the right path to take. A pastor can easily be dragged into the melee and soon you have a split congregation right in the middle of a great campaign. Counsel can help ensure the congregation stays united by taking responsibility for the strategy and addressing any who might have concerns. I for one have never had any congregation member say he or she has worked in more churches than I have, raised more money than I have, and been successful more times than I have. A congregation member may not invite me to

Thanksgiving dinner when the campaign is over, but the member will invite his or her pastor and other church members over, and the church stays united. That is huge! No commander would recommend splitting his forces right in the heat of the battle.

- You want protection against something unforeseen happening. Most often in a campaign events occur that are unexpected. Sometimes these are as tragic as a fire or a hurricane or the death of a significant member or the departure of a pastor. These things happen. If you do not have counsel you will be making decisions around something you have never experienced. Not good! There is a reason army generals have thirty years of experience and are in their fifties. In the heat of the battle you do not want to look to an eighteen-year-old private for instructions. Your counsel has probably experienced just about everything that can happen to you and thus help the church make the right strategic decision to enable victory to still occur.

- You want to make sure you improve the overall generosity of the congregation. Remember, you are in service to God. All that you do is to enable you to grow closer to him. You are fighting an enemy that is striking at the heart of your members every day. You must run a campaign that counters those attacks with the message of generosity and service. Self-run campaigns can actually be treasonous. They can serve the enemy because the emphasis can become money and not transformed generosity, a push to impact the wallet just like the enemy is trying to do instead of impacting the heart for Christ. A well-run capital campaign should and could be the most spiritually challenging event in a congregation's history bringing more persons into a closer connection to Christ than anything they have ever experienced. That is when I say you have had a victory.

I have seen campaigns fail, just as I have seen battles lost. It is not hard with either to look back and see why an outcome did not occur as one had hoped. Failing in either, however, is tragic and with proper planning should never happen. What causes a loss?

- The biggest reason for a loss in battle or the loss of a campaign is NO VISION. There was simply no clearly understood reason for why the church was being asked to do what it was doing. In battle this may be a lack of understanding what the fight had to do with the national interest. A soldier should never have to wonder why he is there. In the church there is not an understanding of what this effort has to do with God's call in our lives.

- The commander is not fully in. If the commander in charge feels that he is being asked to do something that he personally does not want to do, the effort will fail. If a pastor goes along with a church's decision but does not personally feel it is a good thing and does not want to fully contribute, the chance of success drops dramatically.

- There is conflict going on outside of the battle. If the president is under fire politically it will divide the nation on the righteousness of the conflict. If the church is divided over the pastor's leadership it will show up in the support and lack of support for any campaign. It is best to get these issues settled before proceeding.

- History has shown the wisdom of choosing the right leaders. In the Civil War it was widely thought that the Union Army had more troops but poorer generals. The South won many an early battle with fewer troops but superior generals. In a capital campaign the selection of the right leaders can mean a 50 percent increase in success ratio. As in most things, where the leaders lead is where the masses follow. Careful attention to the selection of these leaders is an absolute must for success.

- It is hard to win when trust is lost. If a leader has shown to have abused the troops in the past, it becomes very hard for future troops to trust him enough that they will follow in the present. If a church has held a campaign before and not used the funds secured in the exact manner in which they were raised, serious trust issues will arise that make it very hard for persons to trust enough to commit in the future.

- Hurry is seldom a good idea in anything. Not many generals would just say, "Oh, I see the enemy is over there so let's just run over there and win a battle." However, way too many churches find themselves saying, "Oh, we have a great need and everyone knows about it so let's just have a campaign and fix it." That is a recipe for disaster. They forgo a feasibility study that would allow them to create a solid strategic plan, get the wrong leaders, put together poor communication materials, and just bungle what should have been an easy campaign. Avoid the temptation of hurrying. Do it right.

It was in August that Saddam Hussein invaded Kuwait and President Bush declared that he would not allow that situation to stand. Troops began to go over almost immediately. My own unit was prepped in early fall. Ships began to load up supplies. Planes were set aside to ferry soldiers and marines. In Washington meetings were being held round the clock with generals and admirals putting together a plan of action. September came and then October and December. No fighting had occurred. Finally a date was set for action to start in January, but it was not till February 24 that the big guns of the First Armor Division rolled across the

Iraqi border. But because the planning and advance work was so thoroughly done, it took only one hundred hours for the enemy to surrender and the battle had been won.

Your capital campaign should look much like this. Just because you recognize a great need that deserves attention does not mean you should forgo months of planning and study. When you lay all the proper groundwork and have everything in the right place, once you launch your campaign you will find that victory will come quickly and have a long-lasting effect on the future of your church.

Questions for Review

1. Do you believe your members have accumulated resources available to give or that you have lost many of these gifts over the years for lack of asking for them with a campaign?

2. If you have not had a capital campaign in five years, what might you have one for to give your members a chance to consider a gift from accumulated resources?

3. When reviewing why campaigns sometimes fail do you see anything that may help you understand why your church did not do well previously?

4. Why do you suppose it is so hard for some congregations to consider professional help when something so complex and important is in front of them like a capital campaign? Would your congregation have a difficult time with using counsel?

★ ★ ★

C h a p t e r   1 0

After Action Report

Following the tragic events of 9/11 there was a huge outcry over why we did not act sooner. How could we not have seen what was so plain to see? We had seen embassies blown up, ships damaged, numerous persons killed in terrorist acts. Why did we not take stronger action before that awful day in September? Our defense and intelligence agencies were all asked to file after action reports on exactly what they did and did not do. Somebody was going to be held accountable. These reports were filed and numerous changes made all with the hope that "next time" will be different. And we went to war!

This book has tried to raise the threat level within our churches by saying all the signs are there that we are under attack and that the enemy is only getting more emboldened. In battle after battle for the hearts and souls of Americans the church is losing. Yes, gambling is a huge menace and is a threat. Yes, drug and alcohol addiction is becoming an epidemic and is a threat. Yes, the sexual revolution seems to be destroying what we used to call a family and is a threat. But we will still hold services this Sunday much as

we have for the last hundred years changing very little while act-
ing surprised that said service is getting smaller and smaller.

The biggest threat I see in front of us, and the one we ignore
as much or more than others, is the threat of materialism and our
growing worship of stuff. The serpent is in front of us promising
that if we will only possess this thing or buy that thing or wear this
or charge that, we too will have all that we need to live a wonderful and fulfilled life. We like this idea of controlling our own life
with a credit card and not having to depend upon any God but
Visa and so we bite. Who needs God when you have Mastercard?

But it does not work. We bought and bought and still we feel
empty. We charged to the point that we will not be able to get out
of debtor's prison for fifty years, unless we can just buy this one
more thing. We are addicted to wanting to be like God! This great
sin was the original ruination of the human race and it threatens
us again as never before.

I turn on my phone and what do I see? I see a dozen messages
about how I need to buy this or that today or miss out on a two-
for-one deal. I erase them only to go watch the news on television
and see five minutes of "buy-me" for every ten minutes of information. So I grab my trusty newspaper to scan it and come face-
to-face with a full-page ad for the kind of shoes I must have to
be considered cool and being cool is necessary for my happiness.
It becomes so easy just to surrender to it. Why fight this serpent?
Just eat the apple. Who knows? Maybe I will become like God—
then I will have real victory and I can give myself all the credit.

We are under attack and this attack deserves a decisive and
deliberate response where we give no quarter. We must respond
with a loud and consistent biblical message that generosity is the
best way to fully counter the enemy. When they say take, we say

give. When they say you can have it all, we say we already do in Christ Jesus. When they say keep, we say share. When they say you need more, we say thank you God for the abundance of what I already have. We have to teach a whole new way of being. We have to turn the hearts of persons toward God and away from self. As we begin to move people in this way they will learn and experience the abundant life that generosity brings and become more and more immune to the attack of modern culture.

This will not be an easy battle. We have become lazy and complacent in the church over the years, but our 9/11 is happening. We are losing. We are under significant attack and life as usual will no longer cut it. This is a war, my friends, that we simply cannot lose!

★ ★ ★

Notes

1. The Combat Zone—Area of Operation

1. "See How Your Spending Compares with That of the Average American—and the US Government," CNBC Money, September 27, 2017, https://www.cnbc.com/2017/09/27/how-your-spending-compares-to-the-average-american-and-us-government.html.

2. National Retail Federation, survey, October 28, 2017.

3. "Demographic, Consumer, and Business Data," ESRI, accessed April 13, 2018, http://www.esri.com/data/esri_data/jewelry-map.

4. "Global Gambling Report," Global Betting and Gambling Consultants, June 15, 2017, http://www.gbgc.com.

5. "Internet Pornography by the Numbers; A Significant Threat to Society," Webroot Cyber Security, accessed April 13, 2018, https://www.webroot.com/us/en/resources/tips-articles/internet-pornography-by-the-numbers.

6. George Barna, *America at the Crossroads: Explosive Trends Shaping America's Future and What You Can Do about It* (Grand Rapids: Baker, 2016), 26–27.

7. Barna, *America at the Crossroads*, 29.

8. Tom Radde, "Giving USA: Americans Donated an Estimated $358.38 Billion to Charity in 2014; Highest Total in Report's

60-year History," Giving USA, June 29, 2015, https://givingusa
.org/giving-usa-2015-press-release-giving-usa-americans-donated
-an-estimated-358-38-billion-to-charity-in-2014-highest
-total-in-reports-60-year-history/.

9. "The State of Church Giving through 2012: What Are
Christian Seminaries and Intellectuals Thinking—Or Are They?"
Empty Tomb, October 2014, http://www.emptytomb.org
/research.html.

10. Barna, *America at the Crossroads*, 34.

4. The Rules of Engagement

1. Barna, *America at the Crossroads*, 122.

2. Ibid., 124.

3. Chris Janson, "Buy Me a Boat," by Chris DuBois and Chris
Janson, Warner Brothers Records, 2015.

5. Winning Sure Beats Losing

1. Lyle Schaller, *The New Context for Ministry* (Nashville:
Abingdon, 2002), 161.

2. Herb Mather, *Don't Shoot the Horse ('Til You Know How to
Drive the Tractor): Moving from Annual Fund Raising to a Life of
Giving,* (Nashville: Discipleship Resources, 1994).

7. A Battle Plan

1. http://www.horizons.net/.

2. Dave Ramsey, Financial Peace University, https://www
.daveramsey.com/fpu.

3. Andy Stanley and Lloyd James, *Fields of Gold* (Carol
Stream, IL: Tyndale, 2006); Herb Miller, *Money Is Everything:
What Jesus Said About the Spiritual Power of Money* (Nashville:
Discipleship Resources, 1994); Randy Alcorn, *The Treasure Prin-
ciple, Revised and Updated: Unlocking the Secret of Joyful Giving*
(Colorado Springs: Multnomah, 2017); Mike Slaughter and

Karen Perry Smith, *The Christian Wallet: Spending, Giving, and Living with a Conscience* (Louisville: Westminster John Knox, 2016); Adam Hamilton, *Enough: Discovering Joy through Simplicity and Generosity* (Nashville: Abingdon, 2009); Henri J. M. Nouwen, *A Spirituality of Fundraising* (Nashville: Upper Room Books, 2011).

4. Larry Gormley, "D-Day's Most Famous Photograph," ehistory, accessed April 13, 2018, https://ehistory.osu.edu/articles/d-days-most-famous-photograph.

5. Mike Slaughter, *Christmas Is Not Your Birthday: Experience the Joy of Living and Giving like Jesus* (Nashville: Abingdon, 2011).

8. Special Forces

1. Henri J. M. Nouwen, *Spirituality of Fundraising* (Nashville: Upper Room Books, 2011), 44–45.